LÉON BLOY
the pauper prophet
1846–1917

Emmanuela Polimeni

LÉON BLOY

the pauper prophet

1846-1917

19 47

DENNIS DOBSON LIMITED *PUBLISHERS*

FIRST PUBLISHED IN 1947 BY
DENNIS DOBSON LIMITED
29 GREAT QUEEN STREET
KINGSWAY · LONDON WC2

PRINTED IN GREAT BRITAIN
in 12-pt. Caslon Old Face
BY GIBBS BAMFORTH & CO. (LUTON) LTD
THE LEAGRAVE PRESS LUTON

CONTENTS

CONTENTS

Foreword

'SELDOM has a layman with hands anointed by suffering to the service of God, held up before the world with such a loftiness and sublimity the flaming monstrance of the Faith.'

So wrote Karl Pfleger in his essay on Léon Bloy,[1] the centenary of whose birth occurs this year. (1946 —July 11th). It has taken however, the greater part of a century for this town-crier in God's City to make his voice heard. During his life-time he was subjected to 'a conspiracy of silence', and since his death his worth as a man and as a writer has been but grudgingly recognised. Léon Bloy nevertheless was himself convinced that even though his books never procured him a livelihood, they would live on, and in the final passage of one of his Diaries, 'Le Mendiant Ingrat', he wrote:

Who knows if this pauper may not one day reappear on the verge of that darkness to which men have consigned him, holding in his hand a superb mystical blossom . . . the Flower of the Abyss, the Flower of Silence?

This conviction that posterity would one day do him justice is voiced time and again in Bloy's writings, never perhaps more explicitly than in a

[1] *Wrestlers with Christ* by Karl Pfleger (translated). Sheed and Ward.

chapter of *La Femme Pauvre*[2] where the death of Cain Marchenoir (alias Léon Bloy) is announced.

'Condemned to live apart from the world, he had lived outside it . . . a permanent and terrible menace to a decaying and foul society.'

Yet certain works of his, 'given forth of yore in the chilly void, and deemed by the criminal lunacy of the times to be interred with his bones, were sure to blaze one day and for many a day thereafter into splendour in the startled eyes of a new generation, with the air of a formidable prophecy announcing the end of the latter days'.

Although, as Bloy expressed it, it would then be too late for 'the restorative draught of human kindness to be tendered to those starving, golden lips forever silenced', (for the writer would have passed beyond the justice of men) . . . the times now seem ripe and the moment appropriate to pay tribute to the memory of the author of *The Woman Who was Poor*, to that 'Christian of the Catacombs', whose faith and courage in his own life-time were so inadequately recognised by his contemporaries.

Emmanuela Polimeni

---

[2] *The Woman Who was Poor* (translation) 'La Femme Pauvre'. Sheed and Ward.

I *The Vale of Soul-Making*

IT was on the 11th of July, 1846, in a suburb of the
ancient city of Périgueux, that Léon Bloy first
saw the light of day. Astrologers have found matter
for comment in this fact, tracing certain contradic-
tory features in his character to the conflicting in-
fluences of Saturn and the Sun!

I do not propose to look into *this* aspect of the case,
although it is evident that 'fiery' is about the best
epithet one can apply to Léon Bloy!

Had it not been for his semi-autobiographical novel
Le Désespéré, we would know little of his childhood,
adolescence and early manhood, but it is in the person
of its hero Marie-Joseph-Cain Marchenoir, that Bloy
wishes us to recognise himself, and in the story which
forms the background to the book, his own tragic
experience.

It is true that he transposes and distorts many of
the facts, but his personal reactions to those blows of
Fate which hailed down so unremittingly on his head
are here faithfully portrayed.

In his second novel *La Femme Pauvre*, we are to
hear more of Cain Marchenoir, and after the account
of his death, Léon Bloy makes himself survive in the
person of Leopold, the husband of *The Woman Who
was Poor*.

9

Later on, in his eight diaries, which cover a period of twenty-seven years of married life, we get a more authentic picture of this much-tried writer, and it is these books together with his voluminous correspondence which furnish the data on which we can most safely form an opinion of his religious significance.

From early childhood Léon Bloy seems to have shown that morbid appetite for 'suffering' which remained the dominant trait in his character.

'I was born sad, profoundly, horribly sad', he confessed in a letter to his fiancée, November 21st, 1889, 'and, if I am possessed with the most violent longing for joy, it is because of the mysterious law which attracts opposites. I remember that when I was a very small boy, I often refused with indignation to take part in the games and pastimes the very thought of which made me delirious with delight, because I found it more noble to suffer, to make myself suffer, in renouncing them.' (*Lettres to his Fiancée*). (Lettres à sa Fiancée).[3]

We cannot wonder at his school-mates teasing him unmercifully, nor at his father being asked at last to remove his son from the Lycée, where the unfortunate child had no other weapon of defence save his two strong fists.

In after years he had his vocabulary, a veritable mace that shivered his opponents to atoms, or as one of his biographers termed it 'that cat-o'-nine tails' with which he lashed out at society.

Cain Marchenoir attributed the melancholy and romantic strain in his character to his Spanish extraction, and we do know that Léon Bloy's grandmother came from Aragon.

[3]*Tr.* Sheed-Ward.

That his mother was a remarkable woman with a clear insight into her son's nature, and an understanding of his religious aspirations is evident from Bloy's letters.

Writing to a friend in 1875, he revealed that she had offered to God the sacrifice of her own robust health to obtain the graces he would need to overcome the temptations and difficulties that would surely cross his path.

She, moreover, had dedicated him to Our Lady, asking her to be responsible for his destiny. The story of that destiny shows the extent to which that sacrifice was accepted. Had his mother been spared to him longer (she died in 1877), her wise advice might have helped him in the great crisis of his life.

Léon Bloy's father was a typical bourgeois of the 18th century, a firm believer, however, in religion for the 'family', but far from sharing his wife's ardent Catholicism.

A civil servant himself, his ambition for his son did not rise beyond the thought of an employment which would ensure him a secure living, so when young Léon announced his intention of taking up painting as a career, the father put his foot down firmly.

He would have no child of his joining the ranks of long-haired, half-starved, neurotic-looking youths who frequented the Paris atéliers, and more often than not, finished up in some 'asile de santé' . . . And who can say that such a diagnosis was entirely without foundation?

Léon in an attempt to conciliate his father, agreed to apprentice himself to an architect in Paris who was then engaged in drawing up plans for the new 'Gare d'Austerlitz'. He was then eighteen. We have an extraordinary portrait of him at this age, painted by himself. It depicts a young artist gazing out on an apparently hostile world, the look of perplexed anguish seeming to indicate some inkling of the execrable fate that lay ahead of him. Had Bloy become a painter, it is likely that his pictures would have exhibited many of the features which characterised his writings. His understanding of and sympathy with Rouault's art, his friendship with the painter Henri de Groux, whose immense canvas 'Le Christ aux Outrages' caused much sensation in Brussels, showed in what direction he would have travelled.

As far as we know, Bloy did not seem to have wasted his time, for in his leisure hours we learn that he applied himself seriously to the study of the Classics, and though the idea of becoming a painter was not entirely abandoned, the urge to write was strongly making itself felt. This led him to make the acquaintance of Barbey d'Aurevilly, the well-known author of *Les Diaboliques* and other works.

Bloy has described their informal meeting.

One day, smitten with curiosity, he had penetrated into d'Aurevilly's apartment and, without waiting for an introduction, had blurted out:

'I am told you are M Barbey d'Aurevilly, and having read some of your writings, I thought I would like to have a look at you.'

'Well, sit over there where the light is good' the great man had replied.

'So I sat down', Bloy tells us, 'and in a few days I came back again. After that, I became a daily visitor and this friendship lasted twenty years.'

D'Aurevilly proved to be the one man before whom Léon Bloy willingly bowed, and his influence was no less beneficial to his soul than to his art. By this time he had abandoned the practices of his Faith, and had even developed an active dislike of Catholicism. Barbey was far from being a religious man, although he had an intellectual appreciation of the Church's greatness.

Nevertheless, he managed to inspire his young friend with genuine enthusiasm for the Catholic Faith, and one day during a procession of the Blessed Sacrament in what is to-day the Panthéon, then the Church of Ste Geneviève, Bloy experienced what he claimed to be a thorough conversion.

D'Aurevilly was undoubtedly the instrument chosen to bring this about. 'With an arrow from his bow, he had me pinned down like some barn-owl over the lintels of the Church of Jesus Christ.' Many years afterwards, Léon Bloy fetched a priest to administer to this friend so that he too might die in communion with this same Church of Jesus Christ.

The Franco-Prussian War broke out when Bloy was twenty-four. This campaign proved a rude awakening for France, a moment of stupified astonishment.

Bloy has left us a record of his experiences in *Sueur de Sang*, a work in which were incorporated several short tales of a semi-mystical nature. He dedicated this volume to the man who was made the scapegoat for the defeat of France.

'To François-Achille Bazaine, Marshal of the French Empire, who bore on his shoulders the sins of his country and who, condemned in a travesty of justice, on the testimony of cowardly and disobedient men, had the weakness or rather the heroic generosity not to blight their reputations.'

13

The latter part of this dedication failed to pass the censor!

After the French debâcle, instead of returning to Paris, Léon Bloy spent three years in his native town helping to educate a younger brother, for the family were by now rather badly off. For the first time, he appeared to be relatively happy, his religious fervour had not abated, although in a letter to M Blanc de St. Bonet, the philosopher, we can guess that suffering in some form or other would surely be the pivot around which his life would turn.

'Humanly speaking' he explained to his friend, 'I love everything that is on the grand scale, so it is admirable that God should make me poor; I am full of vainglory, so once again I say it is admirable that I should occupy a lowly position. I love to study, and, at present, I am deprived of all possibility in that direction. I possess, or imagine I possess, one or two exceptionally vigorous faculties, and I am given no opportunity for developing them . . . But, if God has given me apostolic zeal, He will see that I have the means of exercising it, so how can I complain?'

Another letter to a priest at this same time (Bloy is still in his twenties) confirms his desire to lead an integral Christian life.

'When one has reached man's estate, and has accepted in principle any particular truth, the implications of that truth should likewise be accepted. When a man has decided upon a certain course of action, and is neither an imbecile nor a coward, he should pursue the same to the end, or else renounce the undertaking at the start. Valiant hearts do not do things by halves. They do not split truths, taking here and leaving there, they accept them in their entirety and remain faithful to them till death and beyond the grave . . . A semi-rascal rightly inspires one with a certain pity, for error is but an abuse of truth, but the phrase "a semi-Christian" or "a semi-honest man" has no meaning, for here we are dealing with "absolutes".'

In 1873, Léon Bloy returned to Paris and immediately looked up d'Aurevilly hoping that his friend might launch him on his literary career. Unfortunately, the latter was not the man to be of much use to a débutante, he scorned popularity and held himself aloof from the very men who might have been of service to Bloy.

He did, however, introduce him to Louis Veuillot, the editor of *L'Univers* but after having contributed a few articles, only accepted after long intervals, Bloy was told he was 'trop vibrant', and need not return to the office!

Writing about his dismissal to his father he remarked:

I showed too clearly that I worshipped God only, this apparently gave offence.

From now on, began for Léon Bloy that interminable search for employment that would at least keep him from starvation. He spared himself no trouble, and would have been willing to take on any honourable job, although it must be admitted, he was singularly unadaptable. One day, however, happening to see the notice of a vacancy in the Compagnie des Chemins de Fer du Nord, he applied for the post, and was accepted.

The year 1877 opened tamely enough with our would-be man of letters engaged as a railway employee.

Its close was to be anything but tame, for it was during this same year that Léon Bloy embarked on the adventure that was to have for him such tragic significance.

Ever since the day of his religious conversion, he had with unerring instinct sought his rest and happiness in *God*. He had been one of 'Love's conquests', but he had yet to learn to fathom the abysses of the human heart.

It was in the early Spring of 1877, that Léon Bloy came across Anne-Marie Roulé (Véronique Cheminot of *Le Désespéré*), and succumbed to her solicitations.

The following passage from his novel is perhaps the best commentary on the situation.

Suddenly, a revelation of his own affective powers was given to this man chosen to be one of Suffering's elect. He was seized with a craving for human tenderness, coupled with the supernatural longings of a virginal heart.

Christianity had upset the even tenor of his life, and to that famine for Divine Love had been super-added this other famine. How, save by a miracle, could this rapt devotee of the Holy Face, have averted his gaze from those too fragile creatures of clay stamped in the Image of the Divine Countenance, how have escaped this hour of vertigo? (*Le Désespéré.*)

We know little of Anne-Marie Roulé's early life, except that she had received a religious upbringing, that her mother had deserted her in her teens and that a benefactress had subsequently shown a certain interest in her. She had left Brittany about three years before she met Léon Bloy and had come to Paris to eke out her slender earnings as dressmaker by prostitution.

Véronique Cheminot, on the other hand, seems to

have had no such religious upbringing. Bloy speaks of her in *Le Désespéré* as an unfortunate creature 'spawned in an estaminet', brought up in the gutter, polluted since childhood, corrupted at ten years old, sold by her mother when she was fifteen . . .' and known in the Latin Quarter as 'La Ventouse' (the leech).

Anne-Marie Roulé was the first woman with whom Bloy ever had relations. He was then thirty-one. Extreme poverty and a natural timidity had guarded him from temptation till then, but something about this unfortunate creature had made a deep impression on him. He was struck far more by a certain originality he detected in her demeanour than by her looks, and no sooner had he fallen than he was seized with the impulse to rescue her at any rate from the attention of others and to make her give up her former way of living. Anne-Marie in her turn, fell violently in love with the man she gratefully looked upon as her 'saviour', but it was only after heroic efforts on Bloy's part and not a few lapses from virtue, that he was able to emerge victorious from a struggle the strength of which he could never have foreseen.

So successfully however did he convert this Thäis from her evil ways, that there came a day when the erstwhile sinner was outstripping her protector in pious practices, and giving herself up to a life of scarcely interrupted contemplation.

It was during this period that Léon Bloy undertook his first pilgrimage to the Mountain of La Salette where in 1846 (the same year in which both he and Anne-Marie were born), Our Lady is said to have miraculously appeared to two children.

17

Since then 1946 is also the centenary year of this Apparition, it is not irrelevant to recall here the main features of an event which as far as Bloy was concerned, constituted the most important happening of the nineteenth century.

It was on the Eve of the Feast of Our Lady's Transfixion which fell in 1846 on the 19th of September, that two children, Mélanie Calvet and Maximin Giraud having gone to pasture their master's cattle on the slopes of a mountain in the Alps, known as La Salette, were granted an astonishing vision.

Emerging as it seemed from a globe of fire, and seated on a little stone bench, a 'Beautiful Lady' appeared, her face buried in her hands and her whole attitude expressing inconsolable grief. As the children shrank back instinctively, the Lady beckoned them to come near, and, raising her head, whilst 'Tears of Light' coursed down her cheeks, she spoke many mysterious words, the full significance of which has never yet been revealed. After deploring the increasing neglect of God's commandments, especially the profanation and secularisation of the Sabbath and the prevalence of cursing and swearing, she told of terrible things to come because of the volume of men's sins, of homicides in great number, of the din of battle on all sides, and of the earth becoming like a desert . . . The Lady concluded her discourse with a solemn warning that if her People would not repent, she would be powerless to restrain any longer the Arm of her Son from descending in wrath upon them.

'Go, my children, make my words known to *all* my People.'

In spite of the extreme incredulity which this tale evoked in the minds of clergy and laity alike, the memory of this Apparition was not to be effaced.

Every obstacle however was put in the way to prevent the world from knowing the awe-inspiring admonition that a merciful Heaven had given France through the voice of Mary.

Yet in 1851, five years after the event (during which time the children had kept consistently to their original narrative), the Bishop of Grenoble formally pronounced on the validity of the Apparition, and authorised the cult of 'Our Lady of La Salette'. This authorisation only succeeded in provoking renewed hostility, and, although in 1890 Leo XIII ordered a pamphlet to be written in defence of this cause, it was left to Léon Bloy to become its principal champion.

In *La Femme Pauvre* we get the account of this first pilgrimage to a mountain 'as dread as Horeb, where Our Lady of Swords manifested herself in the burning bush of her sorrows'. Bloy spent a night at the shrine.

'When I first got there', he tells us, 'twilight had barely set in. When I rose to my feet, weak as a convalescent centenarian, the night was completely dark, and I could have fancied those were my tears sparkling in the black skies, for I felt as if my roots had been transplanted to the heights.'

It was on this pilgrimage that Léon Bloy first made the acquaintance of the saintly 'missionary', Abbé Tardif de Moidrey, who not only fired his mind with enthusiasm for Our Lady's cause, but initiated him in the mystical interpretation of Holy Scripture. Bloy had hoped to see much of this priest, but he died suddenly in 1879. By this time too he had lost both his parents, Anne-Marie's eyesight was rapidly failing and Bloy himself had rashly given up his job on the railway, the only secure, though very small source of income, he was ever to know. Apart from this deplorable financial position, the life he was leading was exceptionally dangerous from the moral point of view.

Bloy therefore decided to spend a short time with the Trappists at Soligny whilst awaiting the outcome of a proposition by a certain M Puyjalon, who had suggested that both of them should start a paper in Quebec, that the prospects were most alluring, and that in a word, Léon Bloy's fortune was about to be made!

The project of course came to nothing, but during this spell of absence from Anne-Marie, he wrote the letters afterwards to be published by Jacques Maritain as *Letters to Veronica* (1935). In their incredible simplicity and tenderness, they reveal how deeply Léon Bloy felt his responsibility towards his companion. There is no trace of exaltation in this correspondence, but much practical advice and brotherly concern for both her temporal and spiritual welfare.

By now, there had been some talk of marriage, but both parties were at heart averse to this step, Anne-Marie being more determined than ever to lead a contemplative life, and Léon Bloy feeling unable to dismiss from his mind the thought of his friend's past profession. Together these two exceptional souls decided to spend their days in prayer and the study of the Bible, and when Bloy returned to Paris, they gave themselves over to what has been described as 'an orgy of piety'. The physical and mental strain this entailed was soon to show itself. Bloy was made the confidant of 'an amazing secret', the nature and content of which he was never to divulge. To the end of his life, it weighed on his mind, 'a crushing and terrible burden'. It has been thought that Anne-Marie's 'revelation' had some bearing on the role she was convinced that her companion was called upon to play in connection with a further manifestation of the power of the Holy Spirit, and Bloy himself seems to have entertained the belief that he was chosen by God to be one of those 'latter day apostles', of whom he speaks in *Le Désespéré*.

Men, setting hearts aflame with Divine Love, striking at the Devil and his minions with the two-edged sword of God's Word, messengers without gold or silver, mixing with the mediocre in Holy Orders, and with the indifferent laity—moved solely by the zeal for God's Glory and the salvation of souls.

Undoubtedly Bloy gave too material a form to his thoughts in this matter of a future outpouring of the Holy Spirit, although from his writings in general it is evident that his Paracletism was in reality an interior doctrine.

That Anne-Marie was psychically sensitive is most likely, though that she was the authentic prophetess Bloy took her to be is very open to doubt. Ernest Hello and Bloy seemed to have had no scruple in working this unfortunate woman into a state of frenzy in their eagerness to obtain from her interpretations of various passages of Scripture.

In 1882, however, her reason began to give way and she had to be removed to an asylum. Bloy never saw her again, though it was not till 1908, twenty-six years afterwards, that God called this troubled soul to Himself.

21

The years immediately following this disaster were to be the saddest in Bloy's life. Uncertain of his path, engulfed in spiritual darkness, morally weakened and a prey to inconsolable grief, he had nevertheless to think out some way of earning his living. Recognising that after all, his pen was still his best means of support, he now plunged into journalism.

For those able to handle deftly the weapons of irony and ridicule there existed at that time a dis-tinct opening. News-sheets like *Le Chat Noir*, *Gil Blas*, *Figaro* and others, specialised we might say in parody, caricature and mordant criticism.

Bloy joined the staff of one or two of these papers and contributed many articles, some of which were later to appear in book form under such suggestive titles, as 'Propos d'un Entrepreneur de Demolitions'. (Proposals of a Wrecking Contractor), 'Histoires Désobligeantes', (Ungracious Tales), 'Belluaires et Porchers', (To Cattle-drivers and Swine-herds). He even ventured on a little publication of his own, *Le Pal* (the Stake), on which he impaled his victims with evident gusto! *Le Pal* however only ran into four numbers!

Stanislas Fumet, one of his biographers, has spoken of Bloy as 'an Artesian well of maledictions from which it were wise to step aside if one did not wish to be splashed', and has pointed out how the 'Rabelaisian ingredients he so freely mixed with his heavenly intuitions' were most unpleasant to the average reader. Bloy himself admitted that he 'possessed two trumpets, one for the hue and cry, the other for Hosannahs'. It is fortunate that the blasts from the latter were able to drown the echoes of the former, otherwise he would have had an even more limited public!

That he thoroughly disliked his new employ is quite evident from his letters to his friends.

'The very sight of my hideous colleagues caused horror to exude from every pore.' (To Victor Mirbeau.)

And writing later to his fiancée on the subject, he speaks of 'being forced to face the abominations of the world after having bathed in the splendour of God . . . How could my writing be anything but what in fact it was, a vomiting and an anathematising'?

But even Léon Bloy had to admit, 'One fits in where one can', and although this kind of work was not to be permanent, it afforded him great practice in verbal dexterity, so that, when the moment came for him to put his rage red-hot on record, his style was quite formed.

All this time, a project was slowly maturing at the back of his mind. In some dim fashion he knew himself called upon to be the mouthpiece of the inarticulate and the down-trodden of his day, and his sympathies were increasingly going out to all life's dispossessed ones, 'to the disillusioned, the rebels, the damned of this earth'. Surely, he would argue, it was not for nothing that he had been given such a wealth of righteous indignation?

He would write a book, which in the first place must echo his anguish over the long-delayed reign of *justice* upon the earth. For it was God's Justice together with the approach of His avenging Wrath that this modern Jonah thought needed to be proclaimed, even more so than His Love and Mercy. Love is of course the corner-stone of Justice 'for nothing is juster than Mercy, since nothing is more merciful than Justice', but Bloy was also aware that 'a doctrine which proposes the "love" of God as man's final end, needs to be *virile* if it is not to sanction all the illusions of self-love and carnal affection. Time and again, Jesus pronounces his anathemas not on "things" but on "men", whom he designates with frightening precision . . .'

After emphasising that God's clemency hides itself beneath a cloak of justice, Bloy wished to remind and warn 19th century Christians of a few other truths they were in danger of forgetting, for to his eyes, mankind was descending in a spiral movement into a vortex of infamy.

'We are sweeping downwards with no chance of stopping. Each hour we become a little more foolish, a little more cowardly, a little more abominable in the sight of the Almighty Who watches us from the heavenly heights.' This apparently self-assumed role of a denunciatory prophet was not left unchallenged and Bloy had vigorously to defend himself.

'I am told', he wrote 'that I am not qualified to judge nor to punish. Am I then to infer that I am not qualified to *see*? that I am prohibited from lifting my hand against an incendiary who, counting on my fraternal inertia, lights up under my very eyes, the fuse which is to blow up a whole city? . . . What would you think of a man who would let his companions be poisoned, for fear of offending the poisoner? . . .'

In fact Bloy saw himself in a position not unlike the man spoken of in Ezechiel, called 'to set up a hedge and stand in the gap before God in favour of the land that He might not destroy it'. (Ezechiel XXII. 30).

24

The more he pondered on his forthcoming book, the more he wanted to put into it. He was so sick too of literary lies and dramatic catchwords, that he saw here an opportunity for 'boxing the ears of certain littérateurs' whose influence he considered pernicious. But Léon Bloy was fully aware of his own miseries, temptations and falls, and was determined likewise that these should figure in his pages. He gave to his work, therefore, the appearance of a novel and made the interest centre round the story of his own tragic adventure. Finally, to this strange medley of thoughts, he proposed to give the name of *Le Désespéré* (The Desperate Man), explaining nevertheless by means of the sub-title, 'Spem contra Spem', that he did not despair 'theologically' however much he did so 'philosophically'.

He had come it is true, to expect nothing from men, but from God he expected everything. Far from excluding Faith and Hope, Bloy made these virtues the planks of salvation together with that of supernatural charity.

Marchenoir despairs 'with that sublime despair which flings the heart into Heaven, much as the shipwrecked mariner throws his cargo overboard, that he may not be drowned without at least having seen afar the shore of safety'.

Though Bloy was often to experience great elation at the thought of his book, moods of depression easily predominated. He was often to tell his friends of the costly nature of his work. To Mme Henriette Huillier, his confidante and encourager, he wrote at this time :

I am born to be a warrior, a crusader, in an epoch when wars are no longer honourable and crusades impossible. I have dreamed of turning my pen into a sword, yet, I assure you, that if by some miracle I were to become rich, I would leave all this writing and be a servant of the poor. I would deem it a grander and more useful existence to be spat upon by a wretched leper whose sores I was clumsily dressing, than in this Byzantine search for suitable adjectives and participles.

Still, Bloy's artistic talent was such, that what he perceived clearly had to be expressed in language adequately related to the clarity of his vision. As Mme Maritain wrote in her last Memoirs. (*Les Grandes Amitiés*, Vol. 2):

He transformed himself into a loud-speaker so that his message might be carried afar and pierce the walls of indifference, mediocrity and ignorance . . . He had but his 'words' at his disposal, and these he transposed into splendid images and similitudes of the truths he was at pains to broadcast.

These wild and picturesque pages, burning with intense feeling, were dedicated to Louis Montchal, a Swiss Protestant writer, afterwards Bloy's convert. He figures in *Le Désespéré* as Georges Leverdier, Cain Marchenoir's most faithful friend. It was to him personally that Bloy reasserted his unshakable conviction that he was reserved to be the trusted witness of the God of the poor and the oppressed, 'a fact that would be recognised in God's good time'.

'I have the incomparable and miraculous honour to be needed by Him Who has need of no one, and, I have been "salted" by suffering, to stand a very long journey.'

After a certain amount of publicity, on the part of the editor, *Le Désespéré* was launched on the market in 1886.

The walls of Jericho however remained standing in

spite of the blasts which issued from Bloy's trumpet!

The general public were afraid to open what was in reality a social satire, for in this book they scented danger, so true is it that the fear of words often betrays the fears of the truths they express! Bloy's literary colleagues had received such a trouncing that silence was their only dignified refuge. (It is amazing that this writer should have been surprised at the ostracism to which he was subjected by those who, to all appearances, he had gratuitously insulted).

His friends too were aghast at the intensity of his scorn and what they took to be the strength of his hatred. They felt that this book might well be a projectile which would explode in his own hand. What many failed to recognise, was the dominant fact that Léon Bloy only really *hated* there where he could not possibly *love*. He hated mediocrity, because, in the words of Jacques Maritain, 'Mediocrity is one of the modern names for the Evil One'. He hated his epoch, because according to him, it had deprived Charity of its glory.

If others kept silence about this work, Bloy certainly did not. He felt most acutely the bad reception given it and did not hesitate to express his feelings in his letters.

'You speak truly', he wrote, 'when you say that Léon Bloy is ignored and at war with all the powers that be. And why is this? . . . Because he loves Justice above all else, because he is not afraid to voice unpalatable truths, and because he has tried single-handed to start a new current of literature in France, a literature which aims at glorifying Christian spirituality, in opposition to those potentates of Journalism who strive to brutalise and dishonour this

27

generous nation. These men have basely avenged themselves, by shutting all their doors against him, thus depriving him of the means of gaining his bread by his pen and striving to condemn him to silence. The wretched man is forced to spend every hour of the day searching for the bare necessaries of life, thus losing the precious time which he should be using uniquely in literary production.'

And so it was, that for over twenty years, copies of *Le Désespéré* lay about on dusty bookshelves in the Paris libraries, or could have been bought, had there been any buyers, along the quays of the Seine. No editor dared reprint it till 1913. To-day bibliophiles clamour for first editions of a work which has been acclaimed as 'one of the peaks of twentieth century French literature'.

The two years which followed the publication of Bloy's novel were fraught with every form of misery. His courage was fast deserting him and hope was no more than a flicker, all his days were spent in desperate and exhausting expeditions across Paris in search of work. Yet a kindly Providence was nevertheless watching over him, and the day was not far distant when the 'two famines' in Bloy's heart were to be met and his conflicting desires reconciled.

As in a romantic novel help comes to the hero at the psychological moment when he is to succumb to his wounds, so Jeanne Molbech, the daughter of the Danish Lutheran dramatist Christian Molbech came to the rescue of Léon Bloy.

A second milestone in the journey had been reached, but before accompanying our pilgrim further along the road, we do well to pause and cast a glance around at the literary landscape which formed the background to his writings, the more so because Léon Bloy's mission was closely bound up with his literary gifts. God had destined him to be a writer, by brushing aside from him all other means of earning even a meagre pittance. Not that God willed him to *prosper* in that career. The contrary fact just stares one in the face!

Now it is universally admitted that a man belongs to his age before belonging to the ages, and Léon Bloy was no exception to this rule. Most men of letters are influenced for some part of their career by one or other of the literary Schools of their century, and the 19th century in particular was rich in such Schools. Romanticism had flourished with Victor Hugo dominating the scene, though the end of the century saw its decline. When Bloy was only an adolescent, Lamartine, de Musset, De Vigny and others were moving love-sick hearts to tears. Chateaubriand had only been dead a few years. So it was only natural that Bloy too should indulge in rhetoric, exaggeration and the excessive use of hyperbole, all so many recognised devices of the period for attracting readers' attention. Temperamentally if not in his religious outlook, he would be attuned to the Romantics with whom he had a decided affinity, and it is easy to discern in his books his preference for the sonorous phrase and the striking metaphor. When in *La Femme Pauvre* he comments on 'a certain author's style', we feel he is really describing his own. Here he speaks of 'the writer's use of violent colouring, his caustic, elaborated savagery, his whirling, reiterating emphasis, his obstinate unfolding of various cruel pictures that recur persistently, writhing in endless combination like convolvulacious plants . . . the methodically tumultuous crowding of his vocabulary, with its mingling of flames and lava, like Vesuvius in the last days of Pompeii, studied, encrusted, crenelated with antique gems, like a martyr's reliquary . . .' Bloy certainly shared the Romantics' predilection for the bizarre and the occult, and was likewise susceptible to what Baudelaire has termed, 'the charm of horror, which only inebriates the strong'.

The 19th century saw too the rise of the Realist and Naturalist School of writers, and though in one sense Léon Bloy could claim to be included among the first-named group, he made a strong stand against the sceptic naturalism of his day. Zola was honoured with a special publication from his pen—*Je m'accuse*, which took the form of an apology for having on one occasion been so misguided as to pay him a compliment!

Nearly a quarter of the pages of *Le Désespéré* were given up to exposing the mental and moral vices of some of France's most cherished idols.

Léon Bloy, though to some extent plunged into the prejudices of his time, was never imprisoned in his epoch. His rapier-like thrusts against the Rationalists showed him to be a profound believer in France's Christian tradition. All the more reason therefore for the surprise evinced when newly-converted writers like Huysmans and Bourget found themselves almost as bitterly attacked as their irreligious colleagues.

There was some cause however for Bloy's break with Huysmans who had been his companion in adversity for many years. From a letter published in 1934, we gather that the latter had supplied Bloy with 'unverified' information about several of those writers he had attacked in his book.

He utilised me, to avenge himself on some of his enemies whom he dared not attack openly, with no thought of the terrible consequences to me. Most of the aggressive pages in *Le Désespéré* were written on notes he gave me. If Huysmans, in whom I placed infinite trust and who saw more clearly than I did the risks I was running in barring the road to my literary career, had really been my friend, he should have warned me of the danger. (Cahiers Léon Bloy, 1934.)

Yet even so, it would seem as if a break between Huysmans and Bloy would have occurred sooner or later, so totally did they differ in their religious approach. Bloy had his revenge before long, for there is no mistaking whom he intended to portray in Folantin the futurist painter in *La Femme Pauvre*.

He is here described as 'a precious, suddenly discovering Catholicism in a stained-glass masterpiece or a stave of plainchant, going off to the Trappists to be documented on the Aesthetics of Prayer and the Beauty of Renunciation, finding more grandeur in a funeral service than in a Nuptial Mass . . . etc'.

Paul Bourget seems to have been particularly antipathetic to Léon Bloy. He features in *Le Désespéré* as the hard-hearted Alexis Dularier to whom Marchenoir appeals in vain for a trifling sum to cover his father's funeral expenses.

He is also the recipient of the following letter:

You are blissfully ignorant O fortunate novelist of the irony of Fate! Life has been kinder to you than to me. You have the gift of pleasing words, a gift denied to me. No one would ever suspect you of aiming at a literary dictatorship, the very nature of your talent drives away such a thought. You are an amiable and attractive writer, incapable of arousing in your neighbour the spirit of revolt, which it has always been my misfortune to do. Your books in their innumerable editions are seized upon and passed eagerly from hand to hand round in elegant feminine circles . . .

Such a letter would not tend to soften Bourget's heart nor to loosen his purse-strings, and when later he finds himself referred to as a being 'without principles as without passion' and as 'an evangelist of insipidities', it is not surprising that he like many others fought shy of Léon Bloy. We do well to bear in mind however when considering Bloy's evident injustices, and exaggerated comments, that *he* was never to know in the whole of his life what it was to enjoy even that minimum of comfort which is necessary for peace of mind and that he was called upon to make sacrifices for his principles the nature of which his colleagues had never dreamed, yet, whilst *he* was left to starve, these others were being adulated and even venerated as veritable pillars of the Church!

An extract from a letter which appeared on the 21st of January 1889 in *Gil Blas*, proves all the same, that Bloy was not quite unaware of his shortcomings.

My way of writing causes me to make many a rash judgment, and some enormous blunders from which my reputation still suffers. I cried out for instance against certain works which I was only later to understand and appreciate. On the other hand, I exalted to the skies many from which I should have turned away in disgust. Thus it was, that I entirely misunderstood artists like Flaubert and the brothers Goncourt. I was hard on that great poor poet Verlaine, whilst applauding with both hands the writings of a cousin, whom God in His wrath had given me as a relation.

It must be remembered too, that Bloy never set out to be a *literary* critic. He was 'the humble slave of the Holy Trinity and of Our Lady', and it was solely in defence of 'their' outraged names that he drew his sword. If books did not serve God's cause or that of His poor, they must be *bad* . . . It was as simple as all that!

There is no doubt that among all the writers of his epoch, it was Baudelaire, 'that immense poet' as he calls him, who appealed most to Léon Bloy. It was from everyday life that the author of *Les Fleurs du Mal* seized the epic side, and his common humanity comprised the beggars, the castaways, the prostitutes of the great city on whom Bloy had so much compassion. If, as the Goncourts had said 'both language and literature had been formed by men who were too healthy', Baudelaire was certainly an exception, for as a critic has remarked, 'he dowered misery, sordidness, dissolution with a beauty shocking to the vigorous, to the happy, to the optimistic . . . he transfixed in his verse all sorts of fleeting states of mind and body, the fugitive loves and melancholies of men and women'.

We can well understand that Bloy more than Baudelaire's other contemporaries was able to penetrate his thought, pursue his 'dream' and even give it greater plenitude.

The quest for beauty which lies at the root of true Romanticism was uppermost in the hearts of both these men to whom life appeared indeed a 'pilgrimage of pain', but Léon Bloy unlike Baudelaire came early to realise that Beauty, Truth and Goodness, these three, were but different names for the '*One* Absolute', and this discovery was to colour all his thoughts and make of him a promulgator of this Absolute.

Bloy, Baudelaire, Huysmans, d'Aurevilly and the

33

youthful Rimbaud were all captivated in varying degrees with the dark and sinister side of life; a sense of mystery and of the supernatural exerted a great hold on their imaginations and all were deeply conscious of the spiritual reality of evil.

Bloy with his interest in the play of contrasts, realised more fully the truth that only in the *open* conflict with the Light did man become *wholly* aware of the Darkness, and in the Satanic side of existence, he did not fail to see the shadow of the pure Christian light.

It is impossible in a short study such as this one to do more than mention a few of those writers who made the century famous, or who exercised some influence on the work of Léon Bloy, but one more name may perhaps be added, that of Charles Péguy.

The two men strangely enough never met in spite of all they had in common, and the one letter addressed to Péguy by an admiring Bloy remained unanswered.

Nevertheless it was in the apartment vacated by the former when he joined up to go to the front in 1914, that Léon Bloy breathed his last. Both men were great protagonists of the poor and the downtrodden, denouncers of mediocrity and spiritual apathy, devout clients of Our Lady and combators of anti-semitism. Charles Péguy was another great 'neglected' man of his time although to-day his influence is far from negligible among his countrymen.

As the 19th century drew to its close many writers were becoming aware of the spiritual dearth of the hour and of the inadequacy of the Balzacian conception of life based solely on its temporal values, and

34

the first world war was to accentuate this experience. This is not to say that the religious conditions then prevailing in France were of a nature to fill a believer's soul with optimism, but still a revival was beginning to make itself felt, a spiritual discontent as yet but a slight breeze—but sufficiently strong for Bloy to have to admit:

'A new current is at work among us . . . the intellectuals are in search of God, and many no longer fear to ask publicly and openly to know our Lord Jesus Christ, "that most incontestable of all gods" as Baudelaire put it . . . Pharisaism cannot continue to hold sway over men's minds, for the day is approaching when God will vomit from His mouth merely respectable Catholicism.'

Many social injustices deplored by Léon Bloy in his books were being tackled so that the later years of his life were lit up with a hope which was non-existent in his early manhood. In order to gauge however the nature of the difficulties he was up against as an apologist of the Christian cause (for Bloy was more and other than an interesting man of letters), it is indispensable to have some knowledge of the religious background of his times, and some notes of a conference which he was to have made in Quebec in 1879, had the plan to go to Canada materialised, have quite recently come to light.

A couple of extracts from these are worth recording.

At this 'present moment,' the Church in Europe is stretched full length in the mud of our public thoroughfares. She is held up to scorn by those who claim to protect her, she is betrayed by her most loved children—she is deprived nearly everywhere, I do not say of the honours which are due to her, but even of that worldly and superficial consideration which is paid to the most futile of philosophical vapourings.

In fact the 19th century through the voices of its journalists and democratic leaders unanimously proclaim her to be moribund. The most inept apologists of Free-thought and Easy Morality rear themselves in front of her like a pack of savage dogs facing a dying lion. Already the mortal remains of this conqueror of the human race are being disputed and her obsequies prepared. And what obsequies! The most gigantic and diabolically destructive despotism that the world has hitherto witnessed is about to replace Catholicism in Europe—if the terrible Gospel menace is really to be fulfilled, and if the Almighty decides to remove the 'candlestick out of its place' and set it up in other continents. Let those who have remained loyal to the Faith think on these things in fear and trembling.

Léon Bloy continues in a strain which is no less than prophetic as he foresees a great part of Europe experiencing the terrors of mob-rule.

This thing will out at last. Wherever a priest has been uprooted, there springs up a communist.

Such is the law of economic compensation, in virtue of which those commodities for which there is little demand are infallibly replaced by others for which there is even less demand, and which are forced on the public the more tenaciously, the less they are asked for or required. (*Inédits de Léon Bloy*. Editions Serge, Montreal.)

This picture of French religious sentiment is sombre in the extreme even allowing for Bloy's tendency to magnify and dramatise all he touched, and it is highly probable that the religious scepticism engendered in the 18th century had reached its climax about this time, for we know how wide a hearing the Deists and the atheists had obtained in intellectual circles. The positivist doctrines of

Auguste Comte had resulted in the practical deification of the 'human' order and metaphysics had practically been discarded.

Later on, Taine and Renan, though men of contrasting characters, had come to exercise so potent an influence on the minds of Frenchmen that even Christian consciences were troubled. It is true that the French Revolution was partly responsible for many spiritual evils, but this does not nullify Lacordaire's statement that 'had that Revolution been a crime and nothing more than a crime, it would have perished on the scaffold of Louis XVI'. Indeed, one may go so far as to agree with another Frenchman who asserted: 'God saved the Church by sending the Revolution to destroy princely absolutism'.

The Absolute Monarchs and a worldly hierarchy had done much to lower the prestige of the Church in the eyes of the world.

There were also certain 'isms' that were playing havoc in religious circles during the 19th century.

The advent of Modernism had necessitated a very precautionary and in some cases an intransigent attitude on the part of the Church which though amply justified did not tend to peace.

Before the Movement was condemned, it had commanded the allegiance of some of the best brains of the French clergy and of a handful of the laity genuinely inspired by a disinterested spirit, and a single-minded enthusiasm for Truth. The need of a new apologetic which would provide a new defence for the Catholic religion without falling out with what appeared to be certain scientific conclusions had begun to take shape in some minds. However the Modernists had no common body of beliefs, although

37

they were not seeking a solution of their difficulties in the direction of Liberal Protestantism. The majority of the adherents to the Movement remained within the Church after the Papal decrees, for nothing was further from their minds than schism. Time has shown that the Church was justified in her action, but in the 19th century, this could not be clearly seen.

The disputes between the Gallican and Ultramontane elements in ecclesiastical circles, and the decline in the prestige of theology had contributed to the dearth of apologists sufficiently equipped to meet with real success the onslaughts of scepticism. In the beginning of the century laymen like Montalembert and Ozanam and Churchmen like Lacordaire had endeavoured to show their fellow-Christians that there need be no real incompatibility or contradiction between Catholicism and a truly 'liberal' spirit, but the number of such men was insufficient to stem the tide of irreligion and indifference.

So it was that there grew up during the life-time of Léon Bloy that type of Liberalism, ready to tolerate all truths but 'The Truth'.

A more dangerous 'ism' in many respects, because of its extreme subtlety, was that of a 'conservatism' which whilst recognising the social usefulness of the Church, extolling her 'past' achievements, and upholding many of her rulings, pleaded the cause of the Altar primarily in the interest of civilisation and not because of its Divine origin. Many Frenchmen thus mistook their exultation over the Church's greatness for 'Faith'.

Yet none of this unrest, indifference and irreligion which characterised 19th century France need blind us to the fact that lives of exceptional holiness up and down the land were giving God the glory and more than the glory which mediocre Christians denied Him. The country that gave birth in that same century to a Curé d'Ars and a Thérèse of Lisieux had not openly repudiated her title of 'Eldest Daughter of the Church'.

This brief survey of the literary and religious land-scape which formed the background to Léon Bloy's activities, may prepare us better to understand both his writings and his life, the threads of which we now take up again.

II *The Second Milestone*

I T was on a late summer afternoon in 1889, seven
years after Léon Bloy's tragic separation from
Anne-Marie Roulé, that he and Jeanne Molbech
crossed each other's path for the first time. In the
words of the latter, 'We met in the shadow of death',
for Bloy was returning from the funeral of his
friend the poet, Villiers de l'Isle-Adam.

It was not till the next day that Jeanne was
formally introduced to the man known as 'The
Beggar'. He was seated in a corner of the dining-
room of the house of François Coppée, ravenously
eating a crust of bread which he was dipping in a
glass of wine handed to him by Coppée's old servant.

'I came into his life at a time when several of his
friends were mysteriously withdrawing from him as
though he had the plague,' Mme Bloy was to write
later in the Introduction to those *Letters* which
have done so much to shed a light on her husband's
temperament and reveal the ardour of his religious
aspirations. In that one brief meeting two destinies
were sealed. Jeanne Molbech could have had no
idea of the moral worth of that 'beggar' who stood
before her, but she knew him to be no ordinary
pilgrim. 'It was only the grandeur emanating from
him which won me, his ignominy in the eyes of

others that attracted me, his gentleness that ravished my heart.'

Before the end of the afternoon, Léon Bloy had revealed to the young Danish woman many of the secrets of his life, and when she rose to go, she had exclaimed in amazement:

'How is it Sir, that you, a man of such evident superiority, are a Catholic?'

'Most probably just because of that', had replied Léon Bloy.

The next day, Jeanne Molbech received her first letter from the man she was to marry a year later.

I have already mentioned the importance of these letters which were only released to the public in 1921, because as Mme Bloy expressed it, 'Léon Bloy demands it'. She wished his words to go 'as far as that somewhere where an unknown soul awaits them, a soul who will be the "Fiancée of his thought!"'

It is in these pages that Bloy most explicitly and emphatically reiterates what he had only hinted at before, the true reason for that unintermittent poverty and distress which followed him 'along that avenue of cypresses which leads from the womb to the tomb'.

'You know my beloved', he wrote, 'that many years ago, I prayed months on end to be able to suffer for the glory of God. My almost continual prayers were so ardent and impassioned, that I could never give you an exact idea of them.

'I have already mentioned this to you, and, I am sorry to say it all over again, but, you see—it is the *only event of my life that can explain it.*

'God Who knows us perfectly, hears our prayers, and gives us not what we ask but what we need. This fact ought to be the principle of all Christian resignation. I asked Him to let me suffer for my friends and for Him in body and soul. But I had envisaged noble and pure suffering which as I now see would only have been another form of *joy*. I had never dreamed of this infernal suffering that He has sent me and which has consisted in His seeming withdrawal, leaving me defenceless in the midst of my enemies.

'When I made myself responsible for the amazing being whom I have called Veronica, I thought my prayers had been heard, because I suffered daily anguish through the extreme poverty in which I had to support this glorious vessel. But, at the same time, I had revelations and celestial joys such as angels might well have envied. So it was not real suffering. When God took away what He had done me the honour to give me, then I knew what it was to be really unhappy.' (February 15th, 1890.)

When Léon Bloy offered to God the sacrifice of his life, his happiness, his rest, his health, even his intelligence, for the salvation of those he loved who lived away from God, it is probable that in the first place he had in mind Barbey d'Aurevilly, but we learn from his correspondence that he thought too of a childhood's friend, a certain Victor Lalotte, the brother of that Mme Daussin who had commended to him the practice of Daily Communion.

The heroic vow that Bloy made was not always borne in mind, and we find him owning: 'It is true, that I have been treated very hardly, but, I easily forget that once I wanted this to be so. I forget that I asked for this with infinite eagerness and so I lose the merit of my sacrifice.'

Many of the voluntary sufferings which assume

so large a place in Bloy's life were of a very concrete nature. For instance, we learn that abstinence from smoking during a period of thirty-five years to obtain the salvation of a friend, entailed such effort on his part, that it caused him to age visibly, the desire to smoke remaining as strong throughout the thirty-five years as on the day he first took the resolution.

This was the man with whom Jeanne Molbech chose to link her life. Before her marriage which took place in the June of 1890, she had embraced Catholicism, and from now on through her understanding love and exalted piety, became the ideal helpmate for Léon Bloy. How fully he realised his wife's selfless devotion is apparent from the constant references to her in his Diaries.

'She chose to be the companion of a poor man who was universally shunned', he wrote in *Le Pèlerin de l'Absolu*—'to share with him ignominy and calumny, yes—and more than these, had it been the will of God, rather than incur the reproach of having failed to discern the hidden greatness in one of the world's abandoned ones.' Bloy liked to quote this saying of his friend Ernest Hello:

The glory of Charity is to *guess*. He who loves greatness and who loves the outcast will, when passing an outcast, perceive greatness if it be there.

We read in another entry:

It is under my wife's inspiration that I write, guided by her marvellous powers of intuition; it is with joy that I find myself transcribing her very ideas and sentiments.

Materially Bloy's existence was never to improve, though from now on love was never to fail him. Jeanne Bloy understood the meaning of supernatural affection which she described as 'happiness both in time and eternity'. Although her metaphysical gifts enabled her to collaborate in her husband's work, she sank her personality and obeyed lovingly his slightest behest.

'Obedience', she once remarked, 'may prove to be the sepulchre of love, if love has not been its cradle.'

Léon Bloy has referred to his twenty-seven years of married life as 'a poem of grief'.

The wolf of hunger roamed constantly round that little household, and the 'leit-motif' of his Diaries is invariably a cry of anguish.

The following extracts speak for themselves:

(a) I am literally destitute, yet, I would consider myself the vilest of Christians were I to attempt to conceal from others this resemblance to Jesus Christ. Every morning I start out with this thought uppermost—How can I manage to get some food for my family?

Hour after hour, I wander about trying to discern the God of Pity in His heedless creatures. When I think of my terrible plight, it is all I can do not to sin with my lips by uttering words of rebellion. At such moments, so numerous of late, I liken my sad heart to that sponge soaked in vinegar and hyssop which was held up to the Mouth of the Crucified Saviour.

(b) Since Wednesday, my days and nights have been spent entirely in nursing my dear wife and in looking after the two little ones, seeing to their bottles, their clothes and a thousand other things of which I have no experience—I am penniless, full of anxiety and grief, unable to sleep, and I am moreover deprived of my daily Communion without which life for me is nearly unbearable. I am indeed God's anvil in the depths of the abyss, yet I know that it is His love for me that allows all this to happen.

And, after all, the bottom of the abyss makes a good spring-board from which to leap into His Arms.'

The much-tried wife and mother rises to even greater heights. Bloy quotes her as saying on one occasion. 'We draw out sustenance from God's motherly Breast like greedy children with closed eyes, failing to realise the proximity of the Divine Countenance tenderly contemplating us—then, when we do open our eyes and meet that gaze, what a rapturous discovery!'

It is to Mme Bloy also that the following profound reflection is accredited.

'One day, reminding Jesus of our extreme poverty, I said to Him, "Open your Hand Lord, give us what It contains——!" and, Jesus opened His hand, and I saw that It was pierced.'

The thought of the virtue of Hope and its symbol the anchor suggests more symbolism, for Jeanne thinks of the latter as an 'inverted' Cross, 'the Cross cast down from above into the abyss'.

And one day, when there was talk of the family being at last able to leave their squalid surroundings, she was heard to remark gently—'Why should we leave this place? here at all events we are well-known and despised. Elsewhere it might not be so easy to obtain such a grace!'

So passed the first years of Léon Bloy's married life, with his diary recording phrases such as—

'Not a sou left, and nothing to take to the pawn-shop!'

'Lived all day on a salad.'

'No shirt left, no shoes, no hat, no clothes!'

And when things became almost unbearable, he and his wife can still cry out—'All that happens is the adorable Will of God!' They are able to see in the misfortunes that befall them:

45

'Jesus covered with wounds, falling his length on the mud-stained carpet of our souls, imploring us—his friends, not to harden our hearts against Him—and believing this, we are bathed in unimaginable happiness.'

Léon Bloy was thought of and spoken of as 'a beggar', but if, as Barbey d'Aurevilly told him, 'the finest names which men-bear are often those bestowed upon them by their enemies', this epithet was one he could justly be proud of. He could console himself with the thought that after all 'God begs, the Angels beg, the Dead beg, everything in light and glory begs'—why then should he be ashamed to belong to such a goodly company?

And it was for something over and above a meagre pittance on which to live that Bloy begged. It was also for that simple fairplay and justice which were his due, and which men refused to show him; for friendship and for the love of souls. One of the main sources of his grief lay in the fact that what he offered so gratuitously — spiritual nourishment, should have been so scornfully rejected.

In 1897, Bloy brought out *La Femme Pauvre*. It elicited from Maeterlinck the following tribute. 'Monsieur,

'I have just read *La Femme Pauvre*. It is I believe the only contemporary work which shows signs of genius, if by genius we understand certain flashes in the depths which link the seen to the unseen and what is not yet understood with what one day will be. From a purely human point of view, one is involuntarily reminded of King Lear and nothing else comparable to it can be found in any literature.'

In spite of such a eulogy, *La Femme Pauvre* re-

46

ceived scarcely more recognition at the time than did *Le Désespéré*. In this tale of abject poverty and heroic virtue, some of Bloy's own experiences are related, although in this book as in his first novel, the facts are subordinated to the *ideas* the author wishes to express. We are given all the same in these pages as authentic a self-portrait as we can hope to discover, notwithstanding that the striking features in Bloy's character are distributed among or shared by two or three personalities.

We are introduced in the first place to—

'A redoubtable writer—Cain Marchenoir, known amongst us as the "Grand Inquisitor of France", a man who seemed to speak from the depths of a volcano and who brought the Infinite as a matter of course into the most casual conversations.'—In another passage he is referred to as 'a nostalgic contemplative some of whose flashes of perception of what lay behind were uncannily disconcerting'.

Léon Bloy was not unaware of the impression he produced on people. He knew that he 'struck straight at their hearts, and that it was generally looked upon as a hard thing to resist this new Judge in Israel who fought with both hands'.

Cain Marchenoir is further described as 'a contemporary of the last men of the Byzantine Empire— a sort of man of the Middle Ages', or as another writer wrote of Bloy 'a man of the 10th Century who by mistake had strayed into the Third Republic'.

Undoubtedly his piety had a distinctly medieval cachet and he rarely missed an opportunity to proclaim his enthusiasm for that great historical epoch.

In *La Femme Pauvre* for instance we read:

The Middle Ages were a vast Church such as we shall

never more see till God returns upon earth, a House of Prayer as spacious as the whole Western world, built with ten centuries of ecstasy that recall the Ten Commandments of Sabaoth. It was the genuflection of the whole Universe in adoration or in awe—Those men of prayer, those ignorant, unmurmuringly oppressed men, whom we in our idiotic complacency despise, carried the Heavenly Jerusalem within their hearts and minds. Their ecstasies they translated as best they could into the stonework of Cathedrals, into the glowing stained-glass of their chapels, into the illuminated vellum of their Books of Hours—and our whole endeavour when we have some scrap of genius, is to get back to that radiant fountain-head.

No doubt Léon Bloy endowed a greater number of medieval Christians with his own characteristic piety than the actual facts warranted. Yet it cannot be denied, that reprehensible as were many of their *actions*, their 'principles' were sound.

The fear of God, the sense of sin, and the possibility of pardon, were admitted if not always remembered, so that many men whose private lives were public scandals, did not die before making their peace with God.

As Wyndham Lewis, writing of that same period, has told us:

. . . Under the brawl of the streets and the laughing loud song of taverns the screams and giggling of daughters of joy, the everlasting disputations of the Sorbonnical Doctors, the clank of goblets and the clash of steel, the thud of flying feet and the jangle of chains, the creak of ropes on the gallows . . . under all these noises there runs with a steady beat, permanent like ground-bass, the chant of the De Profundis and the Salve Regina . . . (*Life of François Villon*)

Elsewhere Léon Bloy alludes to the Middle Ages as 'a Lent unparalleled in duration'.

To some extent at least, his own life answered to that description, for it was not as a 'sleeper' that he assisted at the Agony of Jesus! Like Pascal, he contemplated that Agony continuing through *time* in the members of Christ's Mystical Body, so that for him as for those medievals 'whose hearts were hot with love', the clamour of the mob still rang in his ears, 'Judas had not ceased to proffer the Traitor's kiss, Peter warming his hands in the hall of the High-priest was repeatedly denying his Master, spittle and blows were still being showered on the Body of Christ, and the abusive shouts of the mob, the sound of the whizzing lash were magnified and multiplied by earth's "present" griefs which rent the air like the clanging of bells in a tempest'. (*Le Salut par les Juifs.*)

Bloy, to whom the tragic aspect of any truth made most appeal, fixed his thoughts where Christianity was concerned, on 'the immensity of Christ's sufferings, on the transcendent horror of the Passion'. He resembled one of his own medievals to whom the sufferings of Jesus were the Bread and the Wine on which they fed.

It is interesting to trace in Bloy's writings the evolution of his moral and spiritual life; when he wrote *La Femme Pauvre* we can already detect the influence of his devoted wife. Remarking on the complete and incredible transformation that 'Leopold' had undergone since his marriage, Bloy explains that this was the outcome of 'a passionate compelling instinct to mould himself on his wife, though no doubt some conflict of his own for which she had been the cue had led him to adopt spontaneously the pious practices of the Watchful Woman of the Holy Book with ever-kindled lamp whom he had married; for

49

H

little by little, he had become a man of prayer'. And in another passage we are told:

Something of great power has tamed this wild creature, suffering, undoubtedly, and some specific suffering—only, it had to be that this potion, this magic philtre should be given him by the hands of the compassionate mistress of spells whose captive he had become.

Even physically there had been a change.

His countenance had preserved its energy, but had sloughed the mask of a soul choked by despair.

When Bloy wrote the above lines however, many hard and bitter years lay ahead of him, serenity of soul had not yet been acquired, and he was to oscillate more often than not between moods of high optimism and deep melancholy.

Bloy reveals to us in *La Femme Pauvre* one of the saddest experiences in his married life, the death of his baby son André, in circumstances similar to those in which 'little Lazare' died, namely the effects of privation and the incredible squalor of his environment. Yet when he reflects on 'the moaning of mothers and the silent surgings in the breast of fathers in the presence of a little child's death', he can offer to Christian parents the consolation that 'something of themselves is surely shining in blissful glory beyond the grave'.

La Femme Pauvre abounds as did *Le Désespéré* in long digressions on Art, Religion, History and other subjects; it also betrays as did his earlier work that same virulence of sentiment which at times soars to the heights of apotheosis, and then as surely makes a spin-dive into those nether-regions where Bloy seems to find a certain pleasure in herding his victims. Many regard this semi auto-biographical work as Bloy's masterpiece; it contains some of his best-known passages and concludes with that most quoted senténce, 'There is only one unhappiness, and that is—not to be one of the saints'.

When Léon Bloy published his second Diary, *Mon Journal* 1896–1900, little André had died, but we learn of the birth of his first daughter Véronique. The family spent two years in Denmark, hoping that there prospects might be brighter. Although lectures and private French lessons brought in a little money, and Mme Bloy's sister lodged with them, we read between the lines that for Bloy's warm Latin temperament, the religious atmosphere of that cold northern land was anything but congenial.

Quatre ans de captivité à Cochons-sur-Marne (Four years of captivity in Pigstye-on-the-Marne), the illuminating title of the next instalment of his journal, 1900–1904—seemed to indicate that things did not improve very much on the return to France. The said 'pigstye' was the little town of Lagny-sur-Marne where the harsh contact with mediocrity in every sphere proved as much a source of suffering as did actual poverty.

The story goes that many years later, Bloy sent a copy of this volume to a friend inscribed '*Sixty* years of Captivity in Pigsties-all-over-the-place'. (*Soixante ans dé Captivité à Cochons-partout.*) The frontispiece in this volume portrayed a bust of the writer executed by the sculptor Frederic Grou. When the original was exhibited in the Paris Salon of 1905, it was placed on a paving stone on which were engraved the symbolic words, 'Léon Bloy on the pavement'. This drew from an onlooker the remark that however long

Bloy remained out in the cold, even on the pavement, he did not belong to the *gutter!*

Since neither his 'books' nor his 'person' could be 'sold', Bloy named the fourth number of his Diary, *L'Invendable*, (1904–1907) and if the French public had its own interpretation to give for the unpopularity of his writings, he too was equally ready to give his reasons.

'There are certain animals', he wrote, 'that can only graze off smooth pastures, others that can reach up to pluck the fruits of the tallest trees. Ridicule me as much as you like, but I am no 'smooth pasture'. God has wished instead to make me a palm-tree, . . . I have had no say in the matter. Each of us is given his own task, each has to speak in his own idiom. Were I to try and harangue the *masses*, I would become impotent, having been created solely to address those who have received a superior culture.'

Bloy once contributed a short tale to the columns of *Gil Blas* under the caption, *Un Homme Bien-Nourri*, the said man being a lean, ill-fed, talented illuminator named Prosper Venard.

It is not difficult to guess to whom Bloy was indirectly and ironically referring, and the anecdote further emphasises his tenacious belief that posterity would alter the verdict pronounced on him by his contemporaries.

'Our lean friend,' so the story runs, 'had a good enough appetite when there was some chance of its being satisfied, although this was less often than people imagined. He was not the man moreover to toady to others. One had great difficulty in persuading him that it was the duty of a penniless artist to make up to any literary freak who had been gracious enough at one time or other to throw out some scraps from his table. Indeed, the greater the artist, the more incumbent on him was this duty.'

'I tried in vain,' wrote Bloy, 'to make out a case in Venard's favour from the *artist's* point of view, but was quickly silenced by those who reminded me that the unsaleable polychromes of this well-nourished man could only hope to prove of interest to a *later* generation, to men living in the LATTER HALF OF THE TWENTIETH CENTURY! a time when according to some prophets, we will see the reappearance of a Charlemagne or a Barbarossa, along with a few dukes who will have emerged from the state of anarchy which will be Europe's in a HUNDRED YEARS or so . . .'

Léon Bloy was constantly being reproached for being obscure, and blamed for being arbitrary and exclusive. To the first class of critic he made the excuse that he had a habit of walking too far ahead of his companions and forgetting that they were out of earshot of what he was saying.

To those who attempted to prove to him how much *more* good he could have accomplished with other methods, he would reply with vigour:

Is it nothing to have saved many souls from Luther's clutches, to have given priests to God's Church, and Spouses to Jesus Christ, to have consoled and reconciled men on their deathbeds, and to have endured for these objects voluntary sufferings? (*Mon Journal.*)

By 1905, Bloy had made the acquaintance of Jacques Maritain, his fiancée Raissa and Pierre Termier, the French scientist, all three of whom became converts to Catholicism and through whose generosity *Le Salut par les Juifs* was later to be re-edited and a book on the Apparition at La Salette,

Celle Qui Pleure published. Of Bloy's remarkable treatise on the destiny of Israel, I will speak later, but *Celle Qui Pleure* though it achieved even less success than his other books claims our attention at this stage in his life.

Ever since he had made his memorable pilgrimage to this holy site, he had been determined to write fully on the subject, but it was not till 1908, thirty years afterwards, that Pierre Termier provided him with the funds necessary to carry out this purpose. Bloy had written to his friend in 1906 concerning this long wait.

'Each day this book is growing within me, and I marvel that after so many years of gestation, it is about to be born in the very hour when the threats predicted at La Salette are beginning to darken the horizon—The time of reckoning is at hand, and there is much to be paid for, much more than one thinks.

'This continual expectation of God-willed catastrophies has become my "raison d'être", the meaning of my destiny and my art. All my roots are bound up in La Salette, and this is why a universal conspiracy of silence has tried to assassinate me:

'My life has been spent in awaiting the Deluge.'

In spite of the little success of *Celle Qui Pleure*, Léon Bloy was not deterred from bringing out in 1912 *La Vie de Mélanie*, an account of the childhood of the 'voyante' of the Apparition, taken from a manuscript purported to have been written by herself at the request of her confessor. From various documents that came into Bloy's possession, and from information obtained from people personally acquainted with Mélanie Calvet, it appears that she

54

was an extremely difficult and complex character, called evidently to lead a life of both mental and moral suffering and to be the victim of much misunderstanding. There seems indeed to have been a striking affinity between the soul of the shepherdess and that of Léon Bloy.

Although he never claimed to have received revelations, both were engrossed in apocalyptic reflections, and had an unusual devotion to the Mother of Sorrows, yet Bloy seems intuitively to have had knowledge of the same facts which Mélanie affirmed were communicated to her in a supernatural manner. It is interesting to know that the latter actually made profession in an English convent in Darlington, taking the name of Sœur Marie de la Croix. Her experiences in England do not appear to have been happy ones and she could not settle down. She was then transferred to a religious House in France which she was asked by the Bishop of the diocese to reform. After one or two more moves, Sœur Marie de la Croix settled in Italy where she died in 1903.

These recollections of her childhood which were all that Bloy published under the title *La Vie de Mélanie* were not written till she was sixty-nine, and it is difficult to assess how much this account was coloured by her later mystical experiences. Those who had access to her in her last years, unanimously bear witness to her holiness of life and to her saintly death. Léon Bloy certainly looked upon her as a kindred soul, and in 1907 wrote as follows to Mme Maritain.

Before Sœur Marie de la Croix expired in darkness and solitude (as was the case with Marchenoir in my novel), this elder sister of mine might well have clasped me in her arms.

55

I hope in my book to depict the tragedy of her exceptional life's history. (*Les Grandes Amitiés*, Vol. 2.)

It was only after her husband's death that Mme Bloy gathering together his remaining notes on La Salette, had them published under the title *Le Symbolisme de l'Apparition*, a work to which she added a valuable supplement.

Between Bloy's diary *L'Invendable* and his next one *Le Vieux de la Montagne* (the mountain in question being that of La Salette), *Le Sang du Pauvre* came out in 1909. This volume contains many profound though obscure reflections on the snare of riches and the self-deception of Dives, but many pages are marred by ultra-violence of sentiment and unnecessary invective.

Between 1912 and 1917 (the year of Bloy's death), his literary output was considerable and included several semi-historical studies. He had always shown himself a keen student of history, and a firm believer in the collective destinies of nations. When in 1912, he brought out his *L'Ame de Napoléon* he was already engaged in 'lovingly scanning God's face in the shadows'.

Convinced of a Divine governance of the world, he was intent on seeking for a pattern which would emerge from the seeming chaos of events, for Léon Bloy held strongly as did Carlyle that 'there is a God's truth in the business of God-created men'. All his historical writings bring out his belief in a rhythm in men's lives, the harmonies of which are concealed, and that room must be left for the play of the unforeseen in the development of human destinies. God has His over-plans, and there is no such thing as *chance*. 'Every man performs freely a necessary act.' (*L'Ame de Napoléon.*) Christopher Columbus for instance, for whom Bloy had almost a cult, was a free agent, but God used 'free' Columbus for the setting forward of his age-long purposes for mankind. The navigator himself had no conception of what the discovery of America would mean for the world. Léon Bloy's *first* work was a plea for the canonisation of 'Le Révélateur du Globe!'

'History,' wrote Bloy, on another occasion, 'is the gradual unfolding of Eternity's landscape before our human eyes. We imagine we see in front of us a vast horizon, whereas in reality we scarcely see three steps ahead. When my friend has turned the corner of the street, I can only envisage him in my memory. I am as separated from him as if he were dead. I know of course, that he exists all the time in God's sight, but, as far as I am concerned, he has disappeared into the abyss . . . That street-corner illustrates any turning-point in history.'

It was in 1915 that Bloy's first 'war' book *Jeanne d'Arc et l'Allemagne* appeared on the market, although he had long sensed the dangers that lay ahead for Europe. His last Diaries, *Le Pélerin de l'Absolu*, 1910–1912, *Au Seuil de l'Apocalypse*, 1913–1916, *Meditations d'un Solitaire* and *Dans les Ténèbres*, either prepare us for, or treat of the first World-war.

Dans les Ténèbres was published posthumously in 1918, and in 1920 Bloy's last thoughts were printed under the appropriate title of *La Porte des Humbles!* He was thinking of some final message when he wrote on the fly-leaf of the last diary to be handed in by him personally to an editor—the following words to Mme Maritain.

My Lady of Compassion has inspired me to write what

is probably my last book. *The Gateway of the Humble* (The Door in the Apocalypse), is so narrow and firmly barred, that I cannot imagine how I shall pass through it. Pray to the Mother who weeps, to transform me into one of those small lizards which are able to creep between 'the clefts of the rock in the hollow places of the wall.' (*Les Grandes Amitiés*, Vol. 2.)[4]

Although Léon Bloy never spared France and voiced many unpalatable truths about her moral state, his patriotism could never be put in doubt. The defeat of 1870 had appeared to him in the light of a deserved chastisement and in *Le Désespéré* he admits—'Yes, we have been thoroughly defeated, and the fact that we are a cowardly, dishonoured and vanquished army throws a light on our intellectual and moral condition'. He lamented indeed over his native land as the Hebrew Prophets wept over the woes of Sion, and likened her capital to 'a City of Shame, seated on the banks of an immense river of vice'.

But when Germany attacked France in 1914, he never doubted that France would this time emerge victorious from the conflict although he evinced little surprise that she was once more engaged with the Hun. For years, he had tried to warn his countrymen of what they might expect. Thus he could write in his journal:

I see the moment approaching, when catastrophe after catastrophe will be the order of the day . . . revolutions one after the other will precede that European anarchy expected alike by the Evil One and the Holy Spirit . . . To-day, those who are not blind should prepare themselves for even greater sufferings than those which befell the Early Christians. The

[4] *Adventures in Grace.* Tr. Longmans, 1946.

modern world is in the clutches of Satan; God will doubtless triumph in the end, but after what days of darkness! All my life, I am repeating this, and people only think me mad.

And when we read in *Jeanne d'Arc et l'Allemagne*, that the struggle in which the continent was engaged was 'but a rise of the curtain, a little interlude before the drama . . .' we need no longer put in doubt that in some dim fashion, Bloy sensed the future sufferings not only of his own country, but of the world in general. Like Amos, he beheld the burden of the nations.

He knew Germany to be by now almost outside Humanity's pale, and his diagnosis of the Prussianised State deserves ample quotation . . . In forecasting its future he maintained—

'Germany will never be brought to her senses till she has sustained a terrible defeat . . . There are some inoffensive kinds of folly, and there are others which are homicidal. German megalomania is of the last species. A military monstrosity has come into being, a new decalogue has been promulgated in which War is declared not only to be inevitable, but desirable, necessary for the physical and moral health of a nation, and a powerful factor in the progress of humanity. For humanity according to this people, is not composed of distinct races, each with its special gifts and qualities, its right to its own life and destiny. Oh no! there is but a hierarchy of 'inferior' races to be governed by means of German militarism and German Kultur. One might almost be tempted to smile in pity at such claims, were it not for the terrible calamities which Germanic pride has let loose upon the world. This people wants but one thing . . . to dominate the world and to crush every-

59

thing that resists it, under the iron heel of Prussian-
ism.'

Léon Bloy believed that no peace with Germany
would be possible till 'Alsace and Lorraine have
been returned to France, and till an independent
Poland figures once again on the map of Europe . . .
till the principles of nationality are taken into
consideration in resolving problems, and till the
German theory that one nation can forcibly seize
another and enslave its inhabitants has been formally
condemned.' (*Jeanne d'Arc et l'Allemagne*.)

There are pages in *Dans les Ténèbres* which might
well have been written by a contemporary of the
recent War.

To hurl oneself fully-armed against nations taken by
surprise, to slaughter thousands and thousands of defenceless
human beings after first torturing them—to burn, pillage
and wantonly devastate the most beautiful lands, to destroy
century-old works of Art, hoping by so doing to bring a
continent to its knees—such is the sole idea of Warfare in
the minds of these Prussianised intellectuals who have
prostrated themselves at the feet of a wretched, third-rate
play-actor.

If from the outset, we had let our revolted consciences
speak, and had let Germany know our horror at her brigan-
dage, if an unanimous cry of indignation had arisen denounc-
ing her turpitude and proclaiming her unworthy to bear
arms, if, I say, the universal stigma of a boundless shame
had been the sole trophy Germany would have borne away
from her foul victories, we might not have 'suffered' less
it may be, but much would have been 'changed.'

The non-recognition of the Germanic conception of
warfare would have brought about a revision of what we
mean by Peace, and a clearer idea and acceptance of the
phrase, 'implacable punishment'.

That the War hastened Léon Bloy's death is probable. He suffered intensely in the grief of others, and mourned the loss of many young friends. A sense of isolation weighed him down and the feeling that he was a 'lost force' often found expression. In *Au Seuil de l'Apocalypse*, he speaks of that instinct for the Absolute which God had given him as He had given in the same way to the hedgehog its prickles and to the elephant its trunk. Bloy was aware that such an instinct involved 'an insatiable and ravenous hunger for what the earth does not contain, and its effect upon its possessor is an unbounded loneliness'.

That loneliness was never more poignantly admitted than in *Les Méditations d'un Solitaire* which a critic likened to a 'great, black catafalque'.

The opening meditation runs as follows:

I am alone. Yet I have a wife and two daughters to whom I am devoted, and who love me dearly. I have god-children whom the Holy Ghost seems to have expressly chosen; I have an exceptional number of true and trusty friends. Nevertheless, I am alone—alone of my kind—alone in God's ante-chamber.

When my name is called, where will all those loved ones be? I know full well that many will be thinking of and praying for me, but still, how far away they will appear! What unutterable solitude will be mine as I face my Judge. The closer one gets to God, the lonelier one feels . . . this is the infinitude of solitude.

Bloy then turns in spirit to all those things which have afforded him consolation in the past—the words of Holy Scripture, the humble Churches and Chapels in which he had so often knelt and offered prayers for the living and the dead. None of these

61

can effectively save him now. He wonders if his guardian angel will not be left shivering outside Paradise like some poor and ill-clad beggar and whether the supplications on his behalf which his friends are offering up will reach Heaven's gate in time.

'I know too well' he reflects, 'that in that supreme moment, not a second will be given me to deliberate on my fate. I shall either be driven forward into God's eternal light, or hurled down into the abyss of darkness.' (*Les Grandes Amitiés*. Vol. 2.)

In the past, Léon Bloy had defended his outbursts of anger as 'the effervescence of his pity': now he has come to realise that 'the ascent to Heaven is best speeded up by contemplation of the Sinless One, and, although disgust and scorn may cause one to flee from evil, a muck-heap is not the best spring-board for the leap into Paradise'.

It was during the October of 1917 that his health gave rise to serious anxiety, and on the 1st of November, All Saints Day, he made his last Communion, all present reciting with him the Magnificat. When two days later he passed away to the sound of the evening Angelus, his death like that of his Blessed Mother resembled nothing more than a gentle 'dormition'. The martyrdom Léon Bloy seemed all his life to have expected had been in his heart only.

'I have spent my life praying for two things, God's glory or death', he made Cain Marchenoir confess in his dying moments, 'perhaps my dilemma has been useless. I am about to be judged, but not by man.

'All those written words of violence with which I have been reproached, will be weighed in a faultless balance, together with the deepest desires of my heart. This much at any rate will be credited to me, that I have longed frantically for Justice, and now hope to obtain that plenitude of joy which God's Holy Word promises will be ours.' (*Le Désespéré*.)

Shortly before his death, Léon Bloy had told his wife that no one but himself could ever know what strength God had put into him for the fight. Now however that the *end* of his arduous pilgrimage was in sight, it was the Infinite in *peace*, the horizon of his true Fatherland that lay stretched out before him.

And when his friend Pierre Termier, anxious to know what his master was experiencing in those last moments which separated him from Eternity, questioned him on the subject—Léon Bloy with a touch of his old vigour and moved by that spirit of eager expectancy which never deserted him, replied, 'A tremendous curiosity!'

They buried him beside his infant son André in the little cemetery of Bourg-la-Reine, outside Paris. A massive granite Cross on whose base is carved the 'Weeping Virgin' of La Salette to-day marks his resting place.

Many were the tributes paid to his memory by those whom he had led to Christ, but perhaps none took more touching a form than the simple wreath laid on his tomb:

'From the Anarchists of Bourg-la-Reine to Léon Bloy, defender of the poor.'

When the author of *Le Désespéré* raised his voice on behalf of the outcast and the down-trodden, when he inveighed against the apathy of the ' bien-pensant', heroism was at a discount, and brutality of expression shocked not only bourgeois ears, but those of the greater portion of his contemporaries.

To-day however, after a paroxysm of suffering has shaken humanity, and a wave of violence all but submerged it, susceptibilities are less well-guarded, and the ultra-respectable or the over-squeamish have, temporarily at any rate, retired into the background of society. Is it too much to hope that some at least of those who have passed through the crucible of war and who are no longer the dupes of shams and semblances, will be more prepared to grasp the significance of Léon Bloy's message than were those of his own generation, and more ready to answer his call to the practice of a more robust Christianity? Was Karl Pfleger mistaken when he so boldly affirmed:

'Spiritual meteors with a core of flame such as Bloy possessed do not penetrate the atmosphere of our planet without setting it on fire sooner or later. Nor are they extinguished so quickly as corporeal meteors, for they come from the depths not of space but of the spirit'?

If Pfleger is right, it is no waste of time to recall those Gospel truths which France's Pauper-Prophet took so much to heart, and which hold good to-day as they did yesterday and as they as surely will to-morrow:

Defunctus adhuc loquitur.

PART II

III   The Man and his Mission

UNLESS the existence of a very definite mission is assumed in the case of Léon Bloy, it is not easy to defend the intransigent attitude he adopted towards his contemporaries, nor at times the methods he employed.

Far from being non plussed by his critics, he would explain:

Were I not known as the 'terrible pamphleteer', nobody would swallow my christian message . . . the form of the pamphlet is for me the armour of the 'missionary'. (*Le Vieux de la Montagne*.)

It is only after having read Bloy's life and penetrated more deeply into his thought that one comes to accept the view that he was not mistaken, and that he had indeed been chosen by God to carry out a formidable task. No single part of his equipment had been given him merely for parade; even his impatience formed part of his armour, inciting him in obedience to a higher call to outstrip the dictates of mere human prudence and speak in the name of the 'Absolute'. Truly a perilous vocation and fraught with moral danger for one whose 'supernatural' indignation was closely allied to a most 'natural' temperamental weakness!

65

Impatience when directed towards individuals is rarely guiltless.

Léon Bloy by the grace of God had been preserved from the temptation to 'partial living', and from the day that he had accepted the Gospel message, had taken as his inflexible rule of conduct the 'Nolite conformari ⬛ huic saeculo'.

Unfortunately his power of apologetic was weakened through his failure to take into account both the concrete conditions which do so much to explain men's actions and those moral and mental endowments with which individuals react to truth.

He considered others only through his own perspective, and was wont to exaggerate the *visible* part of the drama in a Christian soul. This led him to contrast Truth and Error, Virtue and Vice as embodied in human beings in a too sharp and therefore unjust manner. In the language of the Schoolmen, Bloy would have said that he looked beyond *Accidents* to fix his gaze on *Substances*. It was not the man of flesh and bones standing in front of him, nor the actual individual he was recalling who concerned him, but a 'soul' as it would appear on the Day of Judgment, alone before its Maker, shorn of all pretence.

'I am called to occupy a Chair of the Supernatural' was his astounding claim.

And so he set about attacking the supineness, self-complacency, tepidity and worldliness of the 'good' —he let men know that he had come to awaken them from slumber, that he refused to endorse current mediocrity, and that he refused equally to be gagged.

In other words, he preached the re-conversion of the worshipping community!

66

'Why should I have received weapons, if not to fight? why light if not to spread it?' he once wrote to his fiancée. ' . . A misunderstanding on this point would be monstrous and inconceivable, because God does not make fun of His creatures. Oh no! a thousand times no! I have not been misled.' (Letters.)

But where Bloy called for heroism, those around him replied with opportunism. He would argue that his message was no new one, that he did no more than remind men that God is their Sovereign Master, that Christ will one day return in a blaze of glory to judge the world—and that the only wise thing is to be prepared.

He warned his fellow-Christians that the times called for a passionate and not merely a decorous piety, for the final battle would be between saints and deicidal fanatics.

Uncompromising, integral Catholicism, or, as the only other alternative, a world given over to the forces of Evil.

'A Catholic must be not only a torch-bearer, but an incendiary.' (*L'Invendable*.)

Bloy's unalterable belief in the possibility of man's regeneration through the transfiguring power of the Holy Spirit, made it difficult for him not to find matter for censure in the lamentable indifference he saw around him. A miscreant was still a target for God's arrows, but in the persons of tepid Christians the words of Zachariah were confirmed. 'And they shall say to Him, "What are these wounds in the midst of thy hands?" And He shall say, "With these I was wounded in the house of them that loved me"'.

Bloy speaks in *Le Désespéré*, of the 'systematic emasculation of religious enthusiasm through lack of spiritual alimentation'. He maintains that for want of robust instruction, souls become anæmic and sickly, incapable of throwing off the effects of poison in their environment and of assimilating what is good and beautiful.

Time and again, he refers to the need for virile Christians, and arraigns those Catholics who, 'just because they happen not to be out-and-out rogues, are nevertheless so the dupes of the Prince of this world, that they come to look upon themselves as stalwart pillars of the Church! It is impossible to make such men understand that it is just their mediocrity which will bring down God's wrath upon them, and that they will have to face a severe judgment for their absolute indifference'. (Letter to Pierre Termier.)

It was his love of God and the Church which motivated Bloy's condemnations; he thought of so many innocent souls whose early enthusiasms would be damped by pharisaical piety, and who in their youth might be tempted to turn aside from a religion they associated with hypocrisy. No wonder Bloy had some hard things to say about the 'salt of the earth' and its loss of savour!

In the last chapter of *La Femme Pauvre* he returns to this subject. Clotilde (the 'Poor Woman') has been hearing a conventional exposition of the Parable of the Two Debtors, in which 'that indiscreet and inconvenient lesson from the Son of God' had been overlaid with the 'sacerdotal confectionery of St. Sulpice'. Suddenly as in a dream she finds herself listening to the 'real' words which the preacher for the occasion would have liked to have brought home to the complacent congregation,

. . . It is true you have no idols in your houses, you don't blaspheme, the name of the Lord is, as a matter of fact so far from your thoughts that it would not occur to you to take it in vain! On Sundays you pay God the overwhelming honour of your presence. This is the respectable thing to do and sets a good example to the servants. You do not murder with the sword or with poison, that would be displeasing to men and might scare away the customers! Moreover you don't indulge in debauchery in a too open and scandalous manner, you don't tell lies as palpable as mountains, you don't steal on the highways where you might easily be hurt, nor rob banks which are so well-guarded. So much for God's Commandments.

Suddenly the tone is changed, and Clotilde hears an impassioned plea on behalf of God's poor and afflicted ones, who cry unceasingly throughout the centuries . . .

What time is it Father? for we watch without knowing the hour or the day . . . When will this suffering be finished? What is the time by the clock of Your unending Passion? What time is it? . . . 'It is time to pay your rent, or to get out and die in the gutter along with the dogs', replies the Landlord!

And then Clotilde woke up.

There were times when Léon Bloy shed his weight of habitual gravity and indulged in a lighter vein of condemnation, not the less effective for that, and in his two volumes *Exégèse des Lieux Communs*, published in 1902 and 1913, he held up to ridicule the easy morality of stupidity. These criticisms of stock-phrases offered a much needed safety-valve for Léon Bloy's pent up emotions.

His strong sense of humour was able to reach beyond the particular to the universal, and the bourgeois mentality which tries to hide its scarcity

69

of ideas by repeating platitudes, is most wittily illustrated by comments and anecdotes on such slogans as 'Business is Business', 'Nobody is perfect', 'Poverty is no vice', 'I don't pretend to be a saint', etc., etc. But whether Bloy indulges in banter or in denunciations as searing as a red-hot iron, he drives home the same lesson, and brings before the pillory those who temporised with the world, compromised on moral questions or minimised the Gospel message. He looked to the clergy in particular to cherish the super-natural life, and to bear witness to its force and reality for only when this primary duty was conscientiously fulfilled, could one hope to find a laity ready to co-operate with God's Ministers in bringing society more into conformity with His eternal design.

There was a saying of Blanc de St. Bonnet's which he liked to quote:

'A saintly clergy makes a virtuous flock, a virtuous clergy a respectable laity, and a merely respectable clergy a godless people.'

It was the growing laxity among souls consecrated to God's service that met with such severe condemnation at La Salette, and Bloy deemed it his duty to give this due prominence. It was the Apparition of the 'Weeping Virgin' that stirred his soul to its very depths and as the echoes of Mary's voice died away, together with the memory of her tears, he dedicated himself afresh to his task of reminding his generation that if evil was to be defeated, 'good' must be incarnated and find full expression in human lives—principles of themselves do not fight.

Bloy's misfortune was to have been born at a time of an almost catastrophic extension of a mentality the antithesis of his own; but then, he has let us know that he belonged to that category of souls whom nothing could satisfy, whom 'even the sun displeased!' (*La Femme Pauvre*.)

As one turns over certain pages of his books, one inevitably thinks of that other 19th century denunciator of his times—Carlyle, to whom, as a matter of fact Bloy used to refer as 'my literary cousin'. Both men thundered out their message as with a God-given authority, and championed the cause of the poor and the oppressed, convinced that injustice sooner or later would draw down upon itself a nemesis. But Léon Bloy's Bible contained the New Testament, his 'Yea' was devotion to a Person, his experiences led him ever closer to Christ, so that he was able to proclaim with conviction that Love no less than violence had been endorsed by History. Carlyle may have paid a tribute to the 'religion of Sorrow', Christianity was to him only a passing form.

Bloy was far more than a denunciatory prophet, and he was certainly no demagogue. His letters and Diaries throw much light on another aspect of his vocation which has perhaps not been sufficiently stressed.

'Ever since the beginning of my literary career, I have had to content myself with the suffrage of a small minority', he wrote to his friend Georges Schlumberger, after emphasising how his beliefs, sentiments and manner of expressing them had alienated from him the masses, whom he was not 'called' to influence. (*L'Invendable*.)

God had chosen him in particular to speak to minds of 'superior culture', élites in the natural order, whom he wished to inspire with a desire for

Christian perfection, so that a worthy superstructure of Grace might be erected on what was merely 'natural'.

Stanislas Fumet has expressed most fittingly the quality of Bloy's apostolate. He speaks of him as 'an irregular apostle, a converter of intractable souls, of those who want, or think they want, all or nothing.' Bloy takes this tendency into account, and facilitates their conversion by his own luminous demonstration of integral Christianity, by his childlike acceptance of every iota of the Catechism, and his scorn for man's attempts to improve on God and the Church's pronouncements. Souls who instinctively attached themselves to 'absolute' Truth were moved by this Christian who showed it them regardless of their susceptibilities. He discovered to them the mystery of their own abyss. But for him many would still be outside the Church. The dispiriting sight of so many modern Catholics would otherwise have blocked for them the entrance into God's Temple, had not Léon Bloy like a providential Samson broken a way through its pillars'. (*Mission de Léon Bloy*.)

His keen spiritual insight enabled him to penetrate into the recesses of a hitherto little explored world, so that many non-believers were helped to find *inside* the Church what they had imagined could only be found *outside* her shelter.

Since the testimony of Bloy's friends is particularly valuable in assessing the worth of his mission, I propose to invoke here the names of a few of those who claimed his spiritual paternity.

As Jacques Maritain lovingly wrote:

'We who have known the old age of this olive-tree, know too that the "fruit" witnesses to the strength of the sap and the tenacity of the root.'

72

Had it not been for the Maritains, comparatively little would be known in this country about Léon Bloy, but through the publicity given to her god-father's memory in her recent reminiscences, Mme Maritain has aroused a genuine interest in the author of *La Femme Pauvre*, a copy of which book she came across by accident in the summer of 1905.

We read in *Les Grandes Amitiés*, Vol. I, how one day she and her future husband, then young students at La Sorbonne, and both strangers to Christianity, moved more by awe and admiration than by any feeling of idle curiosity decided to beard the 'lion' in his den.

In 1905, Bloy and his family occupied a little bungalow under the shadow of Paris' great Basilica. As soon as the two friends had crossed its threshold, we are told that 'all values seemed dislocated as by an invisible switch'. Intuitively they discerned they were in the presence of a man who far from being a 'whited sepulchre, was rather a fire-stained and blackened cathedral, whose whiteness lay within, in the depths of the tabernacle'.

As they came down from that hill of Montmartre, these young people made up their minds to learn more about the Christian Faith and to learn from one for whom evidently the Gospel message meant so much.

In after years Jacques Maritain would speak of 'the gentleness and tenderness of that "terrible" man and of the marvellous hospitality of that poor couple under whose roof the wings of the miraculous cease-lessly and noiselessly beat'.

For the Maritains often partook of the frugal meals of the Bloy household, because the invitation to share them was so pressing that it was almost im-

73

possible to refuse. The food was of the scantiest, but served with great dignity, and we are told that more often than not,'Léon Bloy's jacket would be buttoned up to the top, since it was evident that he had no shirt'.

No greater tribute could be paid to Bloy's memory than that which recently appeared from Mme Maritain's pen.

'Léon Bloy was born to awaken in men's hearts the sense of the Absolute' she writes in the last volume of her memoirs, 'no less than the meaning of Christ's Passion and the love of the evangelical virtues. Because he "lived" these mysteries, he was able to revive the sense of mystery in others . . . He made us aware not only of his own ecstatic faith, but of the incomparable value of the Faith itself . . . His raison d'être was to produce just that effect in souls'.

And she goes on to affirm 'Nothing during all these years has been able to overshadow or lessen the influence of the invisible presence of our god-father in our lives'.

Shortly after Bloy's death, Jacques Maritain like Stanislas Fumet emphasised once again the unique character of his vocation, which lay in the success he attained with certain souls who 'sought for beauty in earth's dark places, whose minds were too weary and confused to bear the sudden glare of pure doctrine straight away . . . It was such as these who were the most scandalised at the worldliness and infidelity of too many Christians.

'Bloy's method of exposing the Church's doctrines gave them a presentiment of God's glory and brought them out of their night into the radiance of His light'. (Letters.)

Pierre Termier, the French scientist and his daughter Jeanne were among the staunchest admirers and defenders of Léon Bloy. But for Termier, *Celle Qui Pleure* would never have been published, and he came often to his friend's rescue in other ways. 'There were a few of us who felt honoured to pay his rent for him.'

It was this convert of Bloy's who wrote: 'I divide my life into two deeply-separated halves, that which preceded my meeting with Léon Bloy and that which followed it'.

Jeanne was no less anxious than her father to sing the praises of one she felt to be unjustly maligned.

'People reproached him with being hard, bitter and unforgiving, because nowadays nobody is aware what a poem of victory and joy a truly Christian life can be. The sight of mediocre, grubby lives, no longer affects one; to be surrounded by blind souls and loveless hearts, does not fill one with a heavy sadness. On the contrary, every kind of excuse is made to condone apathy. But to one like Léon Bloy who thirsted after absolute realities, a purely rationalising society and a half and half morality were nauseating; this accounts for that salutary scorn to be found in his writings, a scorn which sets the spirit trembling.' (Letters.)

And when ingratitude or parsimony were hinted at, Jeanne Termier would retort:

'Nobody gave of himself more generously or more blindly than the man whom people called "the ungrateful beggar".'

Nobody could be more lost in admiration, more enthusiastic in his appreciations, more sensitive, more quickly disarmed than this dreaded pamphleteer. Throughout his books, we detect that quick response to others' sufferings, that ready sympathy with those artists whom the world neglected or ignored . . .Is there anybody in reality to whom Léon Bloy has not given alms? for to one of his calibre most of us must appear poor and even destitute.

Abbé Cornuau, a retired naval chaplain and one of Bloy's chief correspondents has witnessed no less eloquently to his intrepidity and heroism.

'Léon Bloy is so powerful a writer,' he maintained, 'that after having read his books, certain souls capable of entering into his thought lose their taste for lesser works.

'First and foremost he is an outstanding Christian, that is to say, a friend and follower of Christ; he is a leader, one of those definitely called to bring souls to God and to light up the road to Heaven to men of good-will . . . The Holy Spirit has so blessed his writings that those who read them with understanding cannot fail to grow in love. And if so many modern Catholics turn away from them, it may be because they fear to be caught up in the mechanism of Christian heroism . . . I know many priests who owe more to Léon Bloy than to any of their contemporaries, and who are not afraid to say so. His passion for unadulterated truth has set their minds afire; his tranquil courage in the face of every hardship has cheered their sinking hearts, and his unflinching fidelity and honesty during his long career as a Catholic writer in spite of the pressure put upon him to lower his ideals, has inspired them likewise with that horror of equivocation, compromise and double-dealing which when minimised spells ruin of character. To how many has not Bloy shown the straight and narrow path which leads to the Absolute, along whose borders spring up those perfect Gospel blooms the seeds of which were sown by Jesus in Galilee!'

The effect of example is once again illustrated in Hubert Colleye's *L'Ame de Léon Bloy*.

Colleye was one of those whose faith Bloy had re-vitalised and he describes for us what meeting with him signified in his life.

One day, I met a man marked with a Cross, or rather, he himself was a living Cross, dark yet luminous, a dispenser alike of heat and light. I had the impression of seeing before me an apostle of the first days of the Christian Church, or a Crusader of the First Crusade . . . I had no inquiries about him; to me he symbolised Humanity sauntering through the temporal towards Eternity. I travelled along the road with this man whom nearly all had shunned. Together we climbed the hill from which there is no descent, and as we walked, he opened my eyes . . . for I was blind.

I had the Faith of course, because I had inherited it as one inherits furniture or jewellery. I believed myself to be a Christian, but what kind of Christian is he whose actions are not inspired by the love or glory of God? This man did not 'explain' the truth to me, but he made me realise and love it, he made me see that 'the Beauty of the King's Daughter was all within', he uncovered for me that Beauty, and taught me to distinguish between reality and mirage.

'Come with me' he said, 'for you have much to learn. Christ still suffers in His Body, nor has He ceased to show Himself to the Holy Women. He has ascended to His Father and our Father, whilst remaining in our midst. What is our love when compared with His?' . . . And so this man marked with a Cross showed me the true meaning of life and—I can never forget him . . . (*L'Ame de Léon Bloy*.)

What struck Leopold Levaux, a Belgian writer and also one of Bloy's converts, was his astonishing constancy under affliction. 'God intended him apparently to spend his life suspended as it were from a crane . . . he appeared before us like some monumental, tormented figure, bathed in the light of the supernatural'.

The same Leopold Levaux has left us an interesting tableau of Bloy's surroundings, the study in which he spent his last years. He speaks of the comparative air of comfort which the presence of a well-stocked bookcase, and an imposing bureau (the gift of his father-in-law) gave to the apartment, of the various pictures and portraits on the walls, of the sculptured head of Christ crowned with thorns surrounded by threatening figures of men and women, underneath which were engraved the words:

'And Jesus was silent.'

The Crucifix before which Léon Bloy and Anne-Marie Roulé had so often prayed stood in one corner of the room—a perpetual reminder of a stormy past, and in the centre of Bloy's study was his writing table, which attracted the visitor's notice with its brightly illuminated text, 'Diligentibus Deum Omnia Cooperantur In Bonum'.

A veteran armchair well consolidated with pieces of wire completed the picture.

Pierre van der Meer de Walcheren, a Dutchman, was the Benjamin of Bloy's spiritual children. He has related his impressions in *Journal d'un Converti* to which Bloy wrote the preface; himself, his wife and their two children eventually entered the Benedictine Order.

In his Diary, de Walcheren speaks of the many souls unknown to him who had prayed and suffered for his deliverance, but—'I fancy one is well-known to me—a white-haired man with starry eyes which mirror his soul, a man who loves God above all else and to whom the Church has bound me forever through the indissoluble tie of the Sacrament of Baptism—Léon Bloy, my godfather!'

It was after this conversion that Léon Bloy is supposed to have exclaimed: 'Am I then to act as sponsor to 20th century France? Is it perhaps for this, that I have had to endure such incomparable torments?'

Another friend of Bloy's to whom we are greatly indebted is Mme Isabelle Debran the daughter of that Mme Huillier who was his sympathetic confidante during his most stormy years. Their house was always open to Bloy and his friends and to many poor and talented artists; Mme Debran was instrumental in getting together over three hundred of Bloy's letters and in *Souvenirs et Reliques* quotes from many of them. Here we read of his moments of hope so quickly succeeded by moods of depression, we watch his flashes of joy and listen to his roars of anger, his acts of contrition and his humble thanksgivings. 'He wrote his pages by flickering lamplight, with hunger gnawing at his vitals, with fingers blue with cold, and despair numbing his heart. Like Christ he nailed his message to a cross, "Soul-purification in the furnace of Suffering".' (*Souvenirs et Reliques.*)

Even those writers on whom at times Bloy had frowned could not but recognise, when not blinded by prejudice, his rare qualities. Alphonse Daudet for instance who had been branded as a plagiarist, spoke of Bloy as 'a torchbearer, one who could rekindle the dying embers in a man's soul. There is nothing of the

79

ner or the confessor about him, his is the out-
stretched hand, the sympathising heart, the kindly
welcome, the humble and very human sincerity.'

Before Bloy's death his reputation had spread far
outside his native land; even as far back as 1889,
he had written to Jeanne Molbech:

> Last night I had a visit from a poor young man,
> brought up in Belgium and who had just arrived in Paris.
> He had wanted to see me, having as he expressed it, miracu-
> lously come across me. He knelt at my feet saying: 'You are
> my Christ!' . . . The excessiveness of that word filled me with
> awe, because, who am I to inspire such sentiments? (Letters
> to his Fiancée.)

From all parts of France, from Belgium, Holland,
and Denmark, as far away as Russia, even from
distant Japan, souls whom life had wounded, men
who loved Beauty and Justice and were willing to
fight for them, had come to hear of Léon Bloy and
were anxious to tell of the influence his books had
exercised over them. We hear even a humble lay-
brother Frère Dacien who devoted his spare time to
copying out by hand passages from Bloy's books so
that they might be more widely read.

Many of those to whom this writer appeared in
the light of a deliverer have since died, but there are
a few still alive who will hail the centenary of his
birth with grateful hearts.

And here the name of M Joseph Bollery of La
Rochelle must not be omitted. Up to the outbreak
of the war in 1939, this Frenchman together with
a few colleagues never slackened in their efforts to
keep green the memory of their former friend. At
regular intervals the *Cahiers Léon Bloy* came out full
of valuable information, literary criticisms and notes

80

of conferences on Bloy and his works. Mme Bloy up till the time of her death in 1928, generously contributed to the *Cahiers*, and gave permission for many of her husband's letters to be circulated. She too was convinced that his writings 'would rise again to the surface of contemporary literature like the majestic wreck of some old corsair that has resisted all attempts to sink her'.

M Bollery had likened Bloy to 'a lighted lamp whose flame however much at times it may have flickered and smoked never went out'. Indeed, he endows it still with 'the rescuing power of a lighthouse beacon shining over the dark sea in which the modern world is shipwrecked'.

Testimonies like those from which I have quoted could be multiplied, and have not ceased to come in.

Quite recently an admirer of Léon Bloy drew attention to the fact that the 'conspiracy of silence' which for so long has surrounded his name is now constantly being broken either by an allusion, a quotation, an article or a book, suggested by some current event, generally of a startling nature. Then once again silence reigns, but not before a few more people have heard of France's Pauper-Prophet.

In spite of the undoubted blemishes on Léon Bloy's literary work, and the uncalled-for invective that stains too many of his pages, his writings radiate enough faith, beauty and love to account for the passionate attachment and gratitude of a widening circle of admirers, who are proud to think of themselves as 'Les Amis de Léon Bloy'.

And since it was his intense and dramatic realisation of what is meant by vital and personal religion, that in the first place 'galvanised' his converts and

81

friends, I would like to dwell in the next few pages on this point.

If Léon Bloy looked upon Carlyle as his 'literary cousin', it was to another Englishman that he gave his spiritual allegiance. He spoke of the Oratorian, Father Frederick Faber as 'the greatest ascetic writer of the 19th century'.

We can easily understand that the florid style and the highly emotional character of Faber's books would have appealed to Bloy, but it was a like passion for the conversion of souls, and for the practice of the evangelical virtues, a similar devotion to the Passion of Christ and a deeply filial affection towards His Sorrowful Mother, which established a real affinity between them. Although in many ways, Léon Bloy and Frederick Faber are of yesterday, never was the spirit which animated these two men of 'feeling' needed more than in our times. It was a sentence from one of Faber's works which kept Hope alive in Bloy's heart.

Sorrow is still a form of success for those to whom nothing has succeeded.

Now in making the affirmation that Léon Bloy was a man of deep spirituality, and in particular of Christian spirituality, one has a right to expect to see the virtue of humility put into practice, and it is just here that in the eyes of so many, he was sadly wanting. Indeed, his reputation for arrogance has almost been taken for granted. One wonders if those who so sweepingly have accused him of pride have read those many sorrowful admissions of failure, those bitter self-accusations which crop up time and again in his letters?

Léon Bloy like Peter, wept constantly over his betrayals. When Fréderic Grou the sculptor was engaged on his bust, he reminded the artist not to forget 'to define the furrows, the deep grooves under my eyes'.

'I have wept so much that I am indeed rich', he remarked to Georges Rouault. 'My tears are my only treasure . . . we will be judged by them, for the "Spirit of God always moves upon the waters".' From his fiancée, Bloy hid nothing, she must know every fault and every failing.

It is certain that I despise myself very much, more than you can possibly know or understand.

I know in an absolute way that I am worthless, the things in me that I hold in esteem not being my own . . . I am very childish, and the frailty of my heart is such as to be almost unbelievable in one who has received the gift of intellectual strength and whose words and writing habitually bear the stamp of extreme force.

. . . Yet, I would be a stupid liar if I pretended that I thought myself insignificant . . . Everything good that I could possibly have in me has been given to me and has remained in me in spite of myself, because I have committed such great sins as to banish me from Grace altogether. I have often revolted against God and more often still, I have forgotten His gifts.

Certain acts of my life horrify me.

. . . In reality I know very little, and I have never understood but what God has caused me to understand when I have become like a little child. I am above all—never forget it, an 'adorer', and I have always seen myself as lower than the animals whenever I have tried to act otherwise than by love and the workings of love.

God has given me imagination and memory, nothing else. But my reason is very dull, more or less what the reason of an ox must be, and the faculty of analysis as philosophers understand it, is completely lacking in me. My mother, whom I resemble, applied to me a famous remark which was once made about a great Doctor of the Church.

My dear child, it is true that you are an ox, but an ox whose bellowing will one day astonish Christianity! (Letters to his Fiancée.)

The older Bloy grew, the more humbly he walked before his Maker. The following letter to his friend and admirer René Martineau furnishes but one instance:

A new year has dawned, giving me another occasion for glancing back on the past. The retrospect is not pleasant. I certainly don't cut a fine figure! Let certain people admire me to their hearts' content, that does not alter the fact that at bottom and even on the surface I am rather an unpleasant person.

My one request to those good enough and kind enough to love me, is to bear with me patiently, and to forgive me for the scandal I have given. May they also do their utmost to encourage in others the practice of those virtues in which I have been so sadly lacking. (January 1st, 1913.)

This sense of unworthiness was closely allied with an unbounded confidence in the power of Prayer.

We must pray to endure the horror of this world, pray to be pure, pray for patience. There is no such thing as real despair or bitter sadness for the man of prayer. Believe me, I have the right to speak . . . We must pray simply, foolishly, but with all our will, and pray perseveringly in spite of distaste and weariness, till we experience that inward force which when operative can accomplish so much. (Letters.)

And in one of his diaries, we read:

As for myself, I place nothing above prayer, all that is dissociated from the quest after God means nothing to me. Sentimental objections don't count. The whole question centres round this point. Are we obliged yes or no, to obey the Commandments and Precepts of God and His Church?

84

Mme Maritain once asked Léon Bloy for spiritual counsel. The advice then given would hold good for everyone and at all times.

'However you may be situated', he told her, 'always place the invisible before the visible, the supernatural before the natural. If you apply this rule to the conduct of your life you will be full of strength and steeped in happiness'.

In one of his journals, Léon Bloy traces out for us that journey towards the Absolute, which so well describes his own spiritual attitude. The passage is among those most often quoted.

The Absolute is a journey without return, and that is the reason why those who undertake it have so few companions. Pursuing the same object, marching in the same direction day and night, these pilgrims turn neither to the right nor to the left, be it only on a single occasion and for a single moment . . . Imagine a man of action, an explorer embarking on his travels. His stirring appeal has induced a few ardent spirits to accompany him. But they did not foresee the suffering that lay ahead of them . . . They are led into a desert, a land of desolation. There awaits them cold, darkness, hunger, thirst, boundless fatigue, appalling misery, agony, a bloody sweat. And the foolhardy Leader looks around him in vain for his comrades of the first hour. Then he understands that it is God's will he should bear his sufferings alone, and he plunges into the unfathomable darkness bearing his heart like a torch before him. (*L'Invendable*.)

Bloy's vocation depended for its fulfilment on absolute abandonment to God's Will, which for him was to manifest itself under the form of perpetual anxiety and anguish of soul. Indeed, it would almost appear as if sordid poverty and the sufferings it entailed were a necessity for that fulfilment. Bloy recognised this when he wrote:

85

'My books form one continuous chapter of sufferings. It has not been God's wish that His most fearless witness should have any share in this world's goods; therefore there was nothing to be done about it but to try and draw some profit from this state of affairs and to welcome a poverty which brought me nearer Christ, much as others welcome the riches which draw them away from Him.'

It was because Léon Bloy 'lived' his Christianity in circumstances that might easily have claimed him for their victim rather than as their conqueror, that his words have such an authentic ring.

It is true that some of his beliefs were couched in most unconventional terms, so that it is as well to affirm straight away his religious orthodoxy. Bloy abhorred the very thought of heresy. The Director of the University of Lyons once let fall a hint that some of his statements appeared heterodox.

Bloy immediately demanded reparation for such an indictment on the grounds that this was absolutely necessary for 'a Catholic whose orthodoxy had never up till then been contested'. In season and out of season, he would announce his unswerving devotion to the 'Catholic, Apostolic and Holy Roman Church'.

'Get well into your heads' we find in *Mon Journal*, 'that I belong to nothing or nobody save to God and His Church'.

'. . . Hers is the only bosom for the feeding of mankind'.

Although Bloy was ready at all times to submit his 'intuitions' to the Church's rulings, he was not prepared to take the word of individual theologians on every point of his faith. He knew God's Kingdom on earth to belong to all the centuries, since it was not the construction of any one epoch.

Were there but one Catholic left to pay her allegiance she would still live on with her mysteries, her power and her fecundity. (*Quatre Ans de Captivité.*)

It needs after all but 'one' mirror to reflect the whole of a woman's beauty. (*Le Pèlerin de l'Absolu.*)

Because Bloy exposed certain sacerdotal weaknesses and even enjoyed the sound of an occasional resounding blow, did not mean that he in any way belittled the priesthood. On the contrary. It was his high esteem for the sacerdotal vocation that led him, like it did Karl Adam, to deplore as a great tragedy 'the contrast between the temporal manifestation of God's present Kingdom and its Divine Idea'. (*Spirit of Catholicism.*)

He too would have echoed Adam's statement that, 'An immoral laity, bad priests, bishops or Popes are so many festering and open sores on Christ's Mystical Body.'

It was only natural moreover that the tepidity which he condemned so unequivocally in the laity would assume a far more serious character when exhibited by the clergy.

Never in his zeal did Bloy attempt to usurp those functions which are outside a layman's sphere.

It is Abbé Cornuau who has told us how, after having instructed a convert to the best of his ability, he would lead him to the feet of the priest whom Providence seemed to have pointed out, and then 'leaving him would himself retire into a corner of the church, there to thank God silently and with tears in his eyes for having chosen him to be His ferry-man'.

Bloy revolted against inefficient formalism, but

would never advocate any short cuts to a Christian life which would side step religious practice.

Stanislas Fumet said of him truly:

This irritated, heart-broken soul, who could brook no interference from 'men', drew from dogma and religious practices rigorously observed, that comfort which the whole universe and the world of thought could not procure for him. (*Mission de Léon Bloy*.)

Like his own Marchenoir:

This wild colt never broke away from the shaft nor got loose from the halter. (*Le Désespéré*.)

It is interesting to note nevertheless how closely in many respects Bloy's spiritual outlook and temperament resembled those of an Eastern Orthodox.

In the first place, we find the same conception with its practical implications, of humanity as an entity, the belief in the mystical whole of Creation from which springs the idea of universal solidarity and brotherhood. With Bloy this showed itself particularly in his devotion to the Communion of Saints with its emphasis on the interdependence of the human race. His thoughts on the subject are developed at some length in *Le Désespéré*. Here we are shown how wide is the range of both our good and bad actions, how when one man commits an evil deed or performs a virtuous act, thousands of lives besides his own may be involved, because of the mysterious affinity which exists between certain souls. These sister souls are totally unaware of each other's existence, nonetheless are their actions mutually harmful or helpful.

Bloy was in the habit of offering his sufferings, not for those dearest or nearest to him, but for some hardly-tried victim with whom his soul had such an affinity,

'Every act of charity, every movement of compassion starts a hymn of praise which will resound for eternity' much as an evil deed compromises the whole universe.

And since Jesus is at the centre of all things, and assumes all our burdens, Bloy concludes:

'We cannot strike out at any human being without striking Him, we cannot humiliate our brother without humiliating Him. We cannot vilify, we cannot kill, without injuring Him. The vilest of creatures has to borrow His Countenance to receive a blow, otherwise, that gesture would remain but a gesture, and never reach the Adorable Face that pardons.'

Bloy sees the smallest events in History having their repercussion on the destinies of mankind. What tremendous significance did he then attach to the Apparition of Our Lady at La Salette! His imagination runs riot at the very thought. In his mind's eye he sees 'Thousands of dying and new-born souls wending their way out of Time and into it, experiencing at that moment something of the ecstasy felt by St. John the Baptist in his mother's womb; some are carried along on the irresistible stream of their Advocate's tears to the very foot of the Judge's Throne, whilst others just starting on their earthly pilgrimage, are caught in the ebb-tide of that salutary flow which causes the City of Pride to crumble.

'One day when things hidden are revealed, the real importance of that event which men have chosen to ignore will be recognised . . .'

This idea of solidarity and interdependence in Creation is extended in Bloy's opinion to the animal world.

As man was formed after God's Image and Likeness, animals on the other hand were created in the image of 'Man's reason'. God gave Man sovereignty over the brute creation, and Adam gave to each animal its name. When Man lost his balance, the animals too were involved in his fate, and the immense volume of their suffering forms part of Man's ransom. 'They are held by us as hostages for the Celestial Beauty we have vanquished.'

It is therefore in virtue of the divine animal's arrogance that the precarious happiness of the brute creation was destroyed. From Humanity down to the lowest beasts it would appear that universal pain is one of identical propitiation. (*La Femme Pauvre*.)

The world that Bloy depicts for us is in all respects a 'fallen' one, chaotic, agitated, a world in which nothing is in its right place, where nobody knows his real name, and not until the things which are hidden are revealed, can we expect to understand this groaning universe.

Happiness according to Bloy is always bought by the sufferings of others, it has to be 'paid for' every time, and he asks himself 'Who would do the "paying" were there no longer any poor and suffering ones'? This cosmic consciousness is shared by the Russian orthodox. But this was far from being the only point of contact that Bloy had with his eastern fellow-Christians. He too, like them, looked to the world's salvation through the transforming power of the Spirit. The phrase 'partakers of the Divine Nature' is central in their faith and worship and their idea of salvation is bound up with this 'deification' so to speak of the human race.

Léon Bloy awaited tearfully this 'reign of justice' much as an Orthodox entertains the hope of the repetition on a world scale of the Easter triumph. In Maritain's *The Things which are not Cæsar's*, he stresses the high corrective value of certain Eastern characteristics against the restless preoccupation with material things which marks much of Western Christianity. The Russian Church has never adjusted itself to the spirit of bourgeois society, nor has speculation in the form of theology and philosophy played a role comparative to that which these sciences have played in the West. This is largely due to the fact that the roots of Russian religion have not been in law and order and organisation. Léon Bloy certainly underrated the work of both theology and philosophy in the Church; his mystic soul was too taken up with studying the work of grace in individuals and the spiritual experiences basic to religion, to give much thought to the rational side of his beliefs.

This affinity of soul with the oriental Christian no doubt accounts for the sympathy and understanding Léon Bloy received from a philosopher like Berdiaev, for it is said that out of the whole of French literature, it was Bloy whom Berdiaev studied most deeply and to whose witness he appealed as testifying to his own leading ideas. But where the former would differ entirely from the Russian Christian was in his conception of what is meant by the Church.

Léon Bloy's loyalty to the See of Peter was absolute and he believed unquestioningly in a formal, judicial external authority.

His attitude was based on the historical facts of the Gospel and on the interpretation given them by the Apostles, and not from any temperamental reasons.

Such was the Faith of Léon Bloy, simple and even naive at times, revelling moreover in everything that could enhance the splendour of worship, in music, ritual, and above all in the Church's liturgy. He regarded with loving respect what Sigrid Undset, the Norwegian writer, called 'all those consecrated trifles which the Church offers to her Faithful.'

But it was round the Mass that his devotion centred, and every morning saw him at the altar-rails. During the night he would get up to recite the Office of the Dead.

There is no need to say more of Bloy's love for Our Lady. He was the missionary of her message, the 'knight-errant of her Compassion'. To this his 'sovereign mistress', he would offer 'on bended knees, with tearful eyes and a saddened heart' his *poverty*, his only treasure, a very costly one.

It was because Bloy had this 'real' grasp of what poverty meant as opposed to the merely 'notional' belief in its existence, that his words on the subject deserve to be listened to with attention. Stanislas Fumet has claimed for him the right to be called a 'metaphysician of poverty'. Because he had climbed the rocks, he knew the perils of the rough ascent.

There is indeed scarcely a work of Léon Bloy's that does not touch on this subject, and because this is so, his main thoughts are worth recording.

First and foremost he envisaged the 'mystery' of poverty as incarnate in Jesus-Christ. 'Mendicus Sum Et Pauper.' (Ps. xxx,10.) He could think of God under no other form.

And so it is in *Le Salut par les Juifs* that we find this idea most explicitly expressed.

It does not need exhaustive Biblical research to discover that Jesus Christ was that Poor Man of Whom both Dispensations make mention . . . He was infinitely more destitute than Job on his dunghill, He lacked possessions, . . . He emptied Himself of His glory. Yet, in the midst of destitution He was still God, and it was in the prodigality of His Divine attributes that He manifested His Deity . . . Those who have not experienced the 'election in the furnace of Poverty' of which Isaias has spoken, can understand little of the sufferings of a Passion which continues in the members of His Mystical Body. (*Salut par les Juifs.*)

Given then such an ancestor, the 'poor man' is vested with a special dignity, and can never more be dislodged from his pedestal.

To illustrate and strengthen his argument, Bloy had recourse to Scriptural imagery. His love of the Bible was so great that he 'could never open the Holy Book without experiencing an infinite sweetness, a fragrance, an inebriation which lifted him into the seventh heaven'.

His interpretation of this symbolism was certainly somewhat arbitrary, yet, although he made extensive use of it, he never asked others to affirm, nor did he himself hold as matter for faith, anything that was not contained explicitly or implicitly in the Creeds. His *Sang du Pauvre* is especially rich in flashes of intuition on the subject of Money and the lack of it, although one has to admit that his ideas find little support from the Biblical text. Bloy's reflections are hard to follow since he sees in Money a token both of Justice and of Injustice, of Torment and of Luxury. It is at once execrable and adorable, and 'an outstanding and mobile symbol of the Precious Blood by which mankind was purchased "at a great price" .' Bloy argues that the more men lose their faith in the efficacy of the Saviour's Blood, the more they get to worship its 'symbol'. As atheism increases, so does the thirst

93

and hunger for those 'silver pieces', the barter money for which the Second Person of the Godhead was exchanged.

It was only natural that Bloy should discern in this fact an 'inverted' image of the Eucharistic hunger experienced by the Saints.

Money is also in his eyes 'The poor man's blood', which the rich who are the depository of material wealth prevent from circulating. Instead of utilising it to provide humanity with the necessaries of life and in this way invigorate the whole of society, they withhold it from the great majority, they keep it for themselves. It is against the brazen wall of avarice that the poor beat in vain. 'There are those' writes Bloy, 'who would stifle the desire of the poor man's heart, but this is a criminal attempt to extinguish the smoking flax, and to crush the bruised reed—a violation of that last refuge which Lazarus found in Abraham's bosom'. Such conduct in his eyes, is a direct challenge to the Creator. (*La Femme Pauvre*)

A whole chapter in *La Femme Pauvre* is devoted to the 'mystery' of Poverty.

'The Saints who wedded Poverty out of love and begot many children by her, assure us that she is infinitely lovely.' There are those on the other hand, 'who will have none of such a mate, and die sometimes from terror or despair at her kiss'. Then there is the multitude who 'pass from the womb to the tomb without knowing what to make of such an anomolous entity'.

But in one of his diaries, Bloy has shed a little more light on this question.

'Poverty is in fact a "heaven" for the Saints who

94

chose her, a "cross" for those who do not desire her, but "absolute" Poverty is "hell" . . .'

And here the distinction is made between that poverty which is relative, and is the privation of the superfluous, a condition which can group men together, and that poverty, 'degraded by circumstances, which entails the privation of the necessaries of life, which isolates men and which goes by the name of Destitution'.

Such 'poverty' can never be desired and Christianity alone can accomplish the miracle of helping a man bear its handicaps by promising him future compensation.

'If an unbeliever in the Decalogue and in the Sacraments resigns himself to such poverty' exclaims Bloy, 'then all I can say, is that he must be either an imbecile or a saint'.

Those who lack the necessities of life have a right to claim everything from God, for their poverty is the measure of their need, 'theirs is an emptiness that automatically entitles them to Divine Munificence'.

Salvation for such as these does not offer many difficulties.

'One does not enter into Paradise to-morrow or the next day or in ten years' time but "to-day", if one is poor and crucified', says Clotilde in *La Femme Pauvre*.

Therefore till the fulfilment of the promises contained in the Magnificat, the poor are justified, argues Bloy, in thinking that God's Glory has not been completely vindicated.

It must not be thought, however, that this champion of the poor man's rights despised the rich as

95

such. On the contrary, he reproached those who seemed to imply that Christ came on earth solely for the benefit of those who had none of this world's goods. 'Jesus came for "souls", that is what we should say.' Nevertheless the safety of the rich lies in self-denying almsgiving. Bloy draws for us a picture of the fear that seizes the rich man when Poverty comes too near him. He feels that she is dangerous— 'that the lamps smoke at her approach, that the candles on the banqueting table take on the appearance of funeral tapers—that all pleasure succumbs', and this, because the rich 'sense that Poverty is the very Face of Christ, the Face that was spat upon, that put to flight the Prince of this world, and in the presence of which it is not possible to devour the hearts of the poor to the sound of flutes and oboes'. (*La Femme Pauvre*)

During his life Léon Bloy was made to feel acutely the disgrace of being a 'legitimate' son of Him Who is invoked under the name of Father of the Poor, for his was that 'revolting, scandalous type of poverty that had to be helped, that was connected with no hope of glory and which has nothing to give in return'.

He himself could never resist giving alms when possible, but Charity to deserve the name had to be associated with the Cross. The only time that he ever possessed a comparatively large sum of money was when he inherited on the death of his mother a few thousand francs. We are told that he parted with these almost immediately, only to discover that the recipient of his gift was far better off than himself.

Bloy had not even allowed himself enough money to pay for the registration of his present!

We learn too from one of his diaries that on one occasion, hearing of the pitiable plight of Verlaine, he ran to offer him the few francs he could spare, only to hear afterwards that the smallness of the gift had given offence to the poet.

It was primarily on the *redemptive* part played by human suffering and especially that endured by the poor on which Léon Bloy concentrated his attention. He had no attraction for merely sterile suffering, nor did he look upon it as exercising simply a *useful* role in the world.

He proclaimed it to be 'the vertebral axis of the moral life, the very hall-mark of love'. This made him write to Barbey d'Aurevilly when he was labouring under acute disappointment—'I have become convinced that suffering is the only supernatural element here below, all else is human'.

It was in the repudiation of the *tragic* side of life that Bloy placed his line of demarcation between the bourgeois and the poor. It was in the inability of the latter to deceive themselves with illusory dreams and particularly in their attitude towards suffering wherein lay the great difference between them.

Bloy could only think of the bourgeois as did Browning.

> With ghastly, smooth life dead at heart,
> Tame in earth's paddock as her prize.

Suffering became for Bloy the only means by which he could worthily accomplish his mission and collaborate in the Redemption.

In declaring ourselves members of Jesus Christ the Holy Spirit has vested us with the dignity of co-redeemers of the human race and when we refuse to suffer, we are Simonists and prevaricators . . . When we shed our tears, which are our

97

heart's blood, we shed them on Calvary, they fall first on Our Mother's breast and from thence trickle down over the hearts of all the living.

As members of Jesus Christ and as Children of Mary we can lave the whole world in our tears . . . (*Lettres Inédits*)

Thus is was that Bloy viewed all the Christian virtues taking root in the sweat of Gethsemane and in the Blood of Calvary. There is a striking passage in *Le Désespéré* in which he speaks of the world's Great Penance being inaugurated on that first Good Friday.

For up till that Day, Man had not really understood the full meaning of Suffering. Humanity was not ready for the lesson of the Cross. But when the blood-bespattered executioners came down from the Hill, they spread the news of the Coming of Age of the Human Race. At one bound, Sorrow spanned the gap between Accident and Substance and became Necessity. Then it was that all those Promises of Joy which saturate the Scriptures and which are summed up in the single word 'Beatitude', swept like a whirlwind through the ranks of mankind. Humanity began to suffer in Hope . . . and, this is what we mean by the Christian Era.

Léon Bloy suffered not only from earth's present griefs but in some mysterious fashion from its future sorrows. Like St. Paul he could only preach 'Jesus and Him Crucified'. And when he thought of Mary, it was on the Mater Dolorosa that he fixed his gaze. 'By her Dolours,' Father Faber has told us, 'God hung about her a complete revelation of the great mystery of suffering.'

This 'Knight of our Lady's Compassion' as Bloy called himself, would contemplate the 'Tower of David in sore distress, beleagured by Sorrow as by an armed multitude and refusing to surrender. She is the Citadel of Compassion whose crenelated battlements legions of demons try to conceal from the view of the Faithful, who prefer to think of this resident on Calvary as a sickly-sweet figure set up on a flower-bedecked altar in an azure niche'.

Léon Bloy therefore commiserated with every form of sorrow—with that of the poor on whom God had stamped His image indelibly, with that of Christ, His Mother and His Church. What grief then would not fill his heart when he thought of the sufferings of God's Chosen People, the much-tried Jewish Race?

IV   Bloy and Israel

Léon Bloy first brought out *Le Salut par les Juifs* in 1892, or rather, gave it to a publisher who, in the author's words: 'Suddenly changed his profession and walked off to his new premises with the bales of my unsold copies'. Since Bloy had made no kind of a contract, he had to resign himself to the 'arbitrary sequestration' of what was in his eyes his most important composition. 'The one book I would not be ashamed to present to God.'

In 1905, Mme Maritain came across a copy of this totally neglected work and was so struck with its contents, that she had it re-edited. Bloy was deeply moved by such generosity, and wrote to her:

'You must truly be my sister to have done me this act of charity, for anyone who likes *Le Salut* becomes for me more than a friend. This book is extremely obscure and represents in astonishing abridgement many years of work and suffering . . .' (*Les Grandes Amitiés.*) The new edition came out in 1905 and was dedicated by Bloy to 'Raissa Maritain, written to the Catholic glory of the God of Abraham, Isaac and Jacob'. This little book has by now, thanks to the publicity given it in Mme Maritain's Memoirs, become better known, attention has been drawn to its lyrical and Scriptural beauty, and Mme Maritain has spoken of it as 'a fiery furnace of analogies and symbols which prolong into the infinite the meaning of Divine realities'.

At first sight it would not be taken as the work of a philo-semite and this is true, for Léon Bloy was no 'natural' lover of the Jews.

When treating of the Middle Ages in *Le Désespéré*, he had certainly not spared their feelings.

'The Middle Ages', he had written in 1886, 'had the good sense to confine the Jews in specially re-served kennels, and allowed them to don a distinctive garb, whereby they could be both recognised and avoided. When it was absolutely necessary to have truck with such vermin, one did so on the quiet, and cleansed oneself immediately. The disgrace attached to such contacts, the hazards run in such encounters were the best Christian antidote to a pestilence with which God saw fit to afflict mankind.

To-day, when Christianity is gasping under the heel of its own faithful, people open their eyes wide with astonishment to find the Jews masters of society; and the foremost to evince surprise are just those who have displayed most activity in gain-saying Apostolic Tradition . . . They prohibit the use of disinfectant, and then complain of bugs! . . .'

Bloy modified his sentiments towards the Jews as time went on, so that in 1909, when he alludes to them in his *Sang du Pauvre* he is already on the defensive.

'How could I help bringing in the Jews when writing a book on the poor, for what people are as poor as they? Oh! I am well aware there are the bankers and the speculators. Legend and Tradition conspire to prove that *all* Jews are usurers, and this is readily believed. But I tell you, this is a lie! and concerns only the dregs of Jewish society. Those who know them intimately and are not blinded by prejudice are quick to recognise the all outstanding fact that the Jews are *sufferers*, and bear as scapegoats the bulk of the world's miseries on their shoulders.'

Bloy's main purpose in writing *Le Salut par les Juifs* was to stress that Divine Providence for the accomplishment of some hidden purpose, would not allow the Jews to be exterminated. 'Their history forms as it were a barrier across the life of the human race, like a dam which stems the flow of a current, in order to raise its level. Athwart that current stands the Jew, fixed and immobile; all that can be done is to try and clear this obstacle with the least commotion possible, knowing full well that it cannot be demolished.

There has been no slackening in the effort to do so, but the experience of sixty generations has proved it to be ineffective. Conquerors whom nothing has daunted have tried to exterminate Israel, multitudes who could not forget the affront paid to the Son of God have untiringly acted as its butchers and sought to cleanse the Vine of these noxious parasites.

But this People scattered all over the globe under the tutelage of countless Christian Princes has persisted in the pursuit of its iron destiny, which can be summed up in the one word, 'Survival'.

This stiff-necked, disobedient and perfidious Race, which Moses found so hard to rule has worn out the fury of man. It is an anvil on which all weapons sooner or later have been blunted; it has dented the Sword of Chivalry, snapped in two the finely-tempered blade of the Musulman and broken the cudgel of the mob.'

Léon Bloy sees in Israel a 'Corpus Mysticum' and, with reverential awe he studies the history of this mysterious alien, taking St. Paul as his guide, and finally affirms in glowing language, that the Race which begot the Redeemer will in God's good time be reconciled to Him. In this reintegration of the Jewish race, Bloy recognises a third Age of Christianity.

Le Salut par les Juifs in reality expands the theme put forward by St. Paul in the 11th chapter of the Epistle to the Romans.

If the offence of them (the Jews) be the riches of the world, and the diminution of them the riches of the Gentiles, how much more the fulness of them?

If the loss of them be the reconciliation of the world, what shall the receiving of them be but life from the dead? (Rom. XI, 15.)

Bloy explains how God's promises are without repentance and that the Prophecies of Scripture have never been unsaid.

I mentioned just now that this writer had no 'natural' love for the Jews, he even went so far as to admit that strictly speaking, to love them as 'brethren' could only be accomplished through 'transcendental religion'.

Nevertheless, nothing could gainsay the truth that 'theirs is the immortal stock from which has sprung Our Lord Jesus Christ, a tree stripped and lopped it is true since that "Crucifigatur", but still intact, with its roots inextricably bound up with the designs of Divine Providence'.

This is why anti-semitism in its modern form

particularly, appeared so odious to Léon Bloy. To despise the Jews as a *Race*, was a thing hitherto unheard of!

So from the very start of his book he emphasises that 'the Blood shed on Calvary for Man's redemption, and that which is shed invisibly on our Christian altars is, in the natural and supernatural order JEWISH blood, for that same river which flowed from the five gaping Wounds of Christ had its source in Abraham's bosom'. It was this same thought which had led him to write in *Le Vieux de la Montagne*:

'Supposing those around you never ceased from referring to your fathers and mothers with contempt, and could only speak of them in sarcastic terms, what would be your feelings? Well, that is exactly what happens to our Lord Jesus Christ. People forget, or rather they refuse to remember, that the God-made man was a Jew, the Jew "par excellence", the Lion of Juda, that his mother was a Jewess, the Flower of her Race, that all his ancestors were Jews, not counting the Prophets, and finally, that the whole of our Sacred Liturgy is drawn from the Jewish Scriptures. How convey the enormity of the outrage and blasphemy in this vilification of Israel?'

In Bloy's eyes, it was 'the most horrible of the disfiguring blows received by our Lord in His Passion, the most unpardonable, since it was directed against his mother's face by Christian hands'.

Yet the picture Bloy draws for us of the Jewish people in *Le Salut par les Juifs* is far from flattering, for whilst he is of the opinion that there is no height of sanctity which the Jew could not scale, neither is there any ignominy to which he would not stoop, since he alone fully typifies Humanity, the proletariat of the centuries.

Bloy made much of the play of contrasts. When he wanted to make the light shine out the more brightly, he purposely darkened the shadows. It is true as far as literature is concerned, that the greater density of *evil* offers more powerful possibilities for illustration than does *virtue* taken by itself, and so we often find in the writings of Léon Bloy, the depths invoking the heights: 'The stream of humanity' he tells us in *Le Désespéré*, 'needs a receptacle to give warning by its splash and its stench when aught is dropped from Heaven'. 'Without Barabbas, the Redemption would not have been'.

In the same way he speaks of 'inverted' reflexions, 'inverted' roles.

'The Demons deep down in the chasms of chaos are the inverted reflections of the firebrands of Heaven'. (*La Femme Pauvre*.) Lucifer the Prince of Darkness is the inverted image of the Holy Spirit, the former being the enemy of those in a state of grace, the latter the enemy of bad Christians. So in the early chapters of this treatise, we are given a glimpse of the Jewish market in Hamburg, 'the emporium of the world's refuse', of the 'rabble who swarm about the place like flies on a muck-heap', of three old Jews, to whom Bloy refers as ' "The Ancients", bending shoulder to shoulder over a sack whose fetid contents heaped together for the speedier release of typhus germs, comprised every imaginable object of Semitic bargaining'.

Later on in *Le Salut* Bloy speaks of the 'First Jewish Speculation' and devotes a whole chapter to the analysis of Abraham's 'admirably negotiated amnesty' regarding Sodom. (Gen. XVIII.)

He discerns in the Patriarch a line of conduct strongly reminiscent of the bargaining of any modern Jew, and concludes that:

'In that sublime tabernacle which throughout Eternity will be known as Abraham's bosom, germinated that cockle of malediction which has been so assiduously cultivated ever since.'

Now for ten years Bloy had nourished his soul on the Bible, and it is always to Scripture that he turns to discover clues to the Divine Mysteries, in spite of Solomon's affirmation that 'it is the glory of God to *conceal* the word'. (Pro. XXV.)

Much that otherwise would be completely hidden is partially revealed through Biblical symbolism.

'Each image and symbol taken separately' argues Bloy, 'reveals something of infinite reality; though taken together they act as multi-coloured veils before a single Tabernacle. The texts in which such symbolism occurs, may seem to contradict one another, to be fanciful or incoherent, because at one moment they appear locked in deadly combat, and in the next are united in a loving embrace. Gazed at from a distance, they seem to coalesce into a single whole, only to split up again into isolated units when we attempt to examine them more closely. Although we are aware that these images and symbols are like the several waves of one great ocean, and are powerless to impair Absolute Unity, yet their incessant ebb and flow, their angry lashings one against the other, do confuse and disconcert weak, human intelligence. One has simply to resign oneself to intermittent glances of Divine Truth, remembering how Jesus Who came to fulfil all things, spoke to the multitudes in parables and similitudes.'

Bloy therefore attempts to discover in Scripture the reasons for Israel's age-long chastisement, and though much of his Biblical exegesis appears far-fetched, it none the less calls for attention. Briefly, his argument runs as follows: The Jews were the guardians of the 'written' word, but after they had crucified the 'Living Word', God allowed them to be stabilised in this sacriligious act; they retained a hold on the pale, inanimate metal which symbolised the Word made Flesh. The Jews 'crucified' money, for that was their way of doing away with what was Divine. In other words, they 'meted out to the "Impassible Symbol", the same treatment they had applied to the "Passible Reality". They *exalted* wealth, raising it aloft out of the poor man's reach, as one would hoist a thief upon a gibbet'.

'From henceforth, those "silver pieces", for which God Himself was bartered like a head of cattle, assume a symbolic value, are vested with a mysterious survival power for which Israel stands guarantor. Through a form of blindness which exceeds all other afflictions, yet somehow fails to arouse pity, the Jews, destined to endure till time shall be no more, exchanged this "silver" for the pale figure now expiring on the Cross between two thieves.'

And Jesus called aloud to His Father, 'Forgive them for they know not what they do.'

Bloy ponders on that prayer, and since as he tells us, 'Divine petitions possess a power beyond the ken of man or angel', he imagines that this cry of the dying Saviour would have re-echoed not only throughout the earth, but would likewise have 'reverberated through those gloomy corridors where is stored that metal, of whose dynamic power Lucifer and his rebel angels are so well aware'.

After the Crucifixion which erected as it were a barrier between Money and the Poor, the Universal Church was left with the Poor on her hands, whereas the Jews were left with their tainted silver.

For this, they have been disliked and persecuted down the ages, and because they have become more or less fugitives on the face of the earth, they have been likened to Cain who also slew his brother. But Jacob's posterity would remind the Gentile world that the Lord 'set a mark upon this murderer so that whosoever found him should not kill him'. (Gen. IV, 16.) Israel is aware that between it and God, has been drawn up an everlasting Covenant, which neither side will break.

If it be indeed the Son of God, whom the Jews have crucified, this Saviour of others has only to descend from his Cross and then Israel will see and believe.

But (and here was the dilemma in which the Middle Ages found itself enclosed as in a vice)— Christ *cannot* descend from his Cross, till all the world is gathered round his feet, till the Children of the Circumcision as well, have owned him as their Messiah . . .

It was no wonder that the Medievals felt that the salvation of mankind depended in some inexplicable fashion on the good will of the Jews and that it was mainly through their malevolence that it was delayed!

It is St. Paul who has brought out most explicitly that the revelation of the Sons of God is a matter of *expectation*, that 'we are saved by Hope' and by Hope alone, and that to the 'unspeakable groaning of the Spirit' on our behalf, we too must add our prayers.

Léon Bloy sees in the Parable of the Barren Fig-tree an image of Jewish avarice, inasmuch as when Jesus was hungry, it had not so much as a small fruit to offer him. But the Gospel has warned us that 'it was not the time for figs'. The tree had yet to be dug about. Later on, if it were to bear no fruit, it were time enough to destroy it.

With the words 'Salvation is of the Jews' ringing in his ears, Bloy foresaw the day when the cursed and barren fig-tree, dug about with all this world's ordure, would bring forth the only fruit capable of satisfying the Master's hunger.

Israel's destiny was bound up with the Three Persons of the Blessed Trinity. We note the protection of the First Person, when the Jews were led out of bondage, the inauguration of the Reign of the Second Person through the Crucifixion, finally Bloy affirms that the fulfilment of Israel's vocation will be realised through further outpouring of the Holy Spirit.

It is at this point in his work that we have to remind ourselves that Bloy's statements are not intended to be so many doctrinal pronouncements, but are the reflections of a mystic expressed in such words as he thought would best be grasped by the human mind. He realised only too well the inadequacy of language when it came to speaking about Divine mysteries.

'When one attempts to speak of God and the things of God, all phrases are like so many blinded lions prowling about in the desert in search of well-springs'.

And again: 'How can we poor mortals hope to catch more than fleeting glimpses of the truths contained in Divine Revelation, a Revelation best compared to the firmament when it is overcast by heavy cloud? We can hear the thunder's roll, we can watch the rapid play of the lightning flash as it darts from behind the cloud, it dazzles our eyes—and then departs'.

Bloy may have spoken about the further outpouring of the Spirit in too definite a fashion, and given the impression of some external and spectacular manifestation of His power which is not consonant with the Church's interpretation of the Biblical text, but the real truth which he wished to convey by means of analogies was simply that the Reign of the Holy Spirit (of which as yet we have tasted but the first-fruits) will surely one day come to pass.

After all, the idea of a social reign of the elect among the nations before the Final Judgment finds support among some of the Fathers of the Church and among certain of our modern Biblical exegetes. Satan who will have led nations into apostasy may well be temporarily rendered powerless. The period in history envisaged by Bloy would be thus inaugurated and closed by the Parousia.

It would be preceded by a cataclysm of Love which would change men's hearts into fiery furnaces so that Justice and Mercy would be seen to embrace. It is when Bloy speaks of a *conflict* being waged between Jesus and the Holy Spirit, of the existence of a kind of antagonism within the bosom of the Trinity that he lays himself open to most criticism, although in reality he is only trying to bring home the truth that in a finite and divided world, what in *God* is identical such as Mercy and Justice, must produce here below quasi-fatal oppositions. So he writes:

'From childhood upwards, we are taught that there is that in the impenetrable Essence of God which corresponds to something in ourselves (involving of course no trace of sin), that the tragic synoptic of human sorrow mirrors in some dim and murky fashion a reflection of the stupendous conflagration of Uncreated Light . . . If there is one truth that experience verifies, it is the impossibility of harnessing to the chariot of Humanity the twin steeds of Love and Wisdom; nothing but struggle and strife ensue.'

The 'antagonism' therefore to which Bloy alludes, is but a transitory spiritual one 'in view of the great Love God holds in reserve for His elect'.

There is no doubt that his utterances concerning the Latter Days and the eventual return of Jesus to this earth on a Fiery Cross, were connected with what he took to be Anne-Marie's revelations, although the real nature of this 'secret' to which he so often alludes was never made known.

In a letter to Jeanne Molbech, however, dated October 24th, 1889, he tells her, 'Remember the thing that was revealed to me some time ago and that I alone in the world know', and he proceeds to explain, what he develops at full length in his book, that the Sign of the Cross, 'This sign of sorrow and ignominy is the most expressive image of the Holy Ghost'. In the Cross itself therefore he sees a symbol of the Spirit of Love hidden under an unimaginable travesty. In a Fallen World, even the Paraclete is seen 'as in a mirror', that is to say in such a way that appearance and reality do not correspond.

So the Holy Ghost is not seen as Joy triumphing, but as the 'glory of God like the Jewish Schekhina, weeping in exile'.

Bloy likewise associates with the Holy Spirit the idea of 'extravagance' and by this he means that in all His actions there is something which in human language corresponds to recklessness.

One is aware of something over and above that which one has any right to expect, the word 'surplus' would sometimes best translate Bloy's thought.

For example, if Poverty serves to symbolise Jesus, then Destitution (the excess of poverty) best symbolises the Holy Ghost.

Ignominy again is the surplus of misery, and so can effectively symbolise the Spirit of Love. Jesus espoused Ignominy, for only under outrage does this Spirit shine forth in all its grandeur. The Cross and its Victim are henceforth inseparable.

'Jesus who represents all humanity, bears this Cross which is "bigger" than He.'

The Jews placed this heavy Cross on Our Lord's shoulders, expressly 'that He should experience Love's crushing burden under its hardest form, its most rigid aspect'.

Léon Bloy as we have already said, looked to Love's eventual triumph here below, since he believed in the transfiguration of the universe through the glory of God's adoption.

He looked to the Holy Spirit to bring about the final unification of the human race. But before this would be accomplished, and humanity become 'one' in the luminous Unity of the Triune God, Bloy foretells an increase in the 'abomination of desolation' which will take the form of a wide-spread apostasy among Christians.

In like manner Newman in his generation had this same premonition of a not-too-distant world crisis, which would be characterised by a tide of infidelity sweeping over mankind, and in which the Faithful no less than the unbeliever would be involved.

It was not only in *Le Salut par les Juifs* however that Bloy expressed his fears, for in one of his letters we read:

Either the end is at hand, or all must change. The autumn of this world's days is with us, soul-cultivation is at a stand-still and winter with all its hardships is upon us. . . Still, the indispensable and universal transfiguration which the Spirit of God is able to bring about is beyond the heart of man to conceive.

The seer-like quality of Bloy's utterances finds more and more expression in the final pages of *Le Salut.*

'The Passion will be renewed' he cries out, 'not in the midst of a sullen and detested Race, but at the world's cross-roads, at the ombril of the nations, and the wise will learn that the Gospel of Blood which they thought marked the end of Revelation, is in its turn but another Dispensation heralding the coming of the Fiery Comforter'.

Bloy sees Love's Agony mirrored in the Passion of Israel, and making this same Israel his spokesman, concludes his treatise with these awe-inspiring words:

'Then, the Crucified will descend from His infamous gibbet, symbol of the Liberator Who has been invoked all down the centuries, and the world will learn that I, ISRAEL, have also symbolised that Cross from its summit to its foot

'On ME, Man's Salvation has been fastened.

'From ME, He will descend, for—

' "SALVATION IS OF THE JEWS".' (St. John IV, 22).

What the reactions of Jewry as a whole would be after reading such a tribute to the unique character of its destiny, must remain a matter for speculation, but the following story (the truth of which was vouched for by the narrator), is perhaps worth recording.

'It appeared that one day in February, 1914, a friend of Léon Bloy's was sitting in a café in Tours reading *Le Salut par les Juifs*, when he noticed a stranger looking over his shoulder. He was a very old Jew. When asked whether he knew the work in question, he drew out of his pocket seven small note-books; they contained the Hebrew translation of Bloy's text.

'He then went on to explain how he and his two brothers, one in London, the other in Hamburg, had made a pact to read every week a portion of *Le Salut*. Thus it was, that at the same hour, on the same day, in three different cities, these three Jews read Léon Bloy!'

I have entitled this little book *Léon Bloy, the Pauper-Prophet*. A pauper he undoubtedly was, but is the word prophet a misnomer? In the strictly limited and popular acceptance of the term—yes!— though evidently even in his lifetime there were found those who spoke of Bloy as a prophet.

That he himself laid no claim to the title is seen in a passage from *Le Salut* when he explains to his

114

readers that he regrets sincerely not being able to pose before them as 'an authentic revealer of secrets', for he has not had the honour of being 'entrusted with consignments of future events'.

He is even more explicit in his journal when he writes:

If people will ironically or not, bestow that name on a vociferator of my type, they must accept the consequences inherent in the very nature of things, namely, that his cries will have the power of accelerating calamities. A prophet above all else is a voice which calls down Justice. (*Quatre Ans de Captivité.*)

Yet in a sense Bloy, like Dante, Pascal and Newman possessed gifts which can be associated with the work of prophecy in the Church, and which are not necessarily confined to prevision and prediction. All 'supernatural' truths by the very fact that they are 'in God' can be thought of as *distant*, the more so, since Truth is one and indivisible. Men like the above-mentioned, were chosen to bring certain aspects and implications of those eternal truths more vividly before the minds of their contemporaries. Gifted with great intuitive insight, they shared in common an impression of impending catastrophe, which largely contributed in making them each in his own way, a disturbing element in society.

The most striking quality of Bloy's mind was this insight into those truths which lie so to speak just 'beyond' reason. And it was this 'intuitive' intelligence coupled with spiritual sensitiveness and magnificent energy which compensated for the lack of reasoning power and sense of proportion that are noticeable in his writings.

He seemed incapable of sustained argument.

But then it must be remembered that it is the evanescence of all intuitions that make the expression of them so difficult.

A man's personal experiences hold for himself the secret of the vital, but are bound to lose much of their purity and simplicity when formulated; the distortions and disproportions occur in the attempt to transpose those experiences into the world of sense. Léon Bloy's enlightenment was solely the gift of Grace and in no way the outcome of an intellectual 'tour de force'. One must never expect to find in his works the tabulated reasoning of a philosopher, nor the methodical approach of a man of science. It seems almost ironical that this despiser of strict logic and this contemner of Science should have had as godsons Maritain the Thomist and Termier the geologist! 'Yet, if', as Fumet put it, 'rationalists hammer at the intellect, Léon Bloy produced tremors of the soul' and it is T. S. Eliot who has reminded us that 'the greatest proofs of Christianity for others, is not how far a man can logically *analyse* his reasons for believing, but how far in practice he will stake his life on his belief'.

Bloy staked his life on the hypothesis of Faith, and the demand came to him as we know, not in the form of martyrdom but in the daily sacrifices that were asked of him and in the voluntary sufferings he endured for souls.

Yet it is no uncritical cult that one would wish to advocate for this 'volcanically supernatural Catholic'.

His personality, his actions and his books were not without serious blemishes, which his enemies were only too ready to seize upon to discredit him in the eyes especially of religiously-minded people. Those inspired by envy or hatred did not hesitate to level such charges against him as those of being a scatological writer, a mystic sensualist, a charlatan, a beggar and an 'ungrateful' one at that. Not the least cause of his unpopularity lay however in the fact that he announced impending disasters to a profoundly optimistic society. A man who spent a life time contradicting his own century, convinced that in so doing, he was fulfilling a mission, could only succeed in annoying his contemporaries. One whose work dealt so much with disconcerting anathemas could never be 'popular'.

That is why Léon Bloy shocks or dazzles far more than he pleases. He is not an 'attractive' writer.

'Only those who love me "supernaturally" can hope to understand me' he once wrote in his diary.

But, even 'supernatural' love is not just to be had for the asking! Those who differ too widely from him in temperament and outlook are bound to feel alienated from him. This being the case, the advice proffered by Stanislas Fumet may prove as wise as any.

Ascertain carefully your reactions towards Léon Bloy. If his writings appear to lead you away from God, close your book, and keep quiet about him. It is unlikely that you will be asked to share with him hereafter the same heavenly mansion! (*Mission de Léon Bloy.*)

It is related that Veronica Bloy when quite a small child, defending her father's somewhat impetuous admonitions to his co-religionists, remarked, 'but then Father is the sheep-dog of the fold!'

Nevertheless, it is among the sheep of the same fold, that Léon Bloy is likely to remain a sign of contradiction.

It was his friend Pierre Termier who in spite of his unbounded admiration for his work, which he compared to 'an immense Byzantine mosaic, marvellously homogeneous, magnificently of one piece as was his life—' spoke of him as 'a generous wine covered with foam which needed skimming before being drunk'.

It is certain that time must still do its work in sifting and appraising among the many volumes of Bloy's literary output.

To use another metaphor, like an over-luxuriant tree, he needs to be pruned. And yet, while awaiting that this labour of love be accomplished, and that fuller recognition be given him in the world of letters, one can hasten his free entry into the world of *souls*. According to the treatment meted out to his writings, in which after all Léon Bloy survives, this is speeded on or delayed.

It is therefore not primarily as a denunciatory prophet to which I have wished to draw attention in this brief appreciation of Léon Bloy and his writings.

If I have succeeded in awakening some interest in this 'immoderate genius', it is not that readers' ears should be strained not to miss one blast from his trumpet, but rather that they should be attuned to catch the echoes of those tears and prayers which this pitiful lover of souls so unceasingly offered up for friends and enemies alike, and whose faith in the Gospel verities led him to look upon the absence of sanctity among the professed followers of Christ as the world's major disaster.

Principal Works of Léon Bloy

Le Désespéré (The Desperate Man), 1886.

Le Mendiant Ingrat (The Ungrateful Beggar), 1891–1895. 1st Diary.

Salut par les Juifs (Salvation through the Jews), 1892. 1st Edition. 2nd Edition 1905.

Sueur de Sang (The Bloody Sweat), 1893. Experiences of 1870.

Mon Journal (My Journal), 1896–1900. 2nd Diary.

La Femme Pauvre (The Woman Who was Poor), 1897.

Exegèse des Lieux Communs (Analysis of Stock-phrases), 1902. 1st Volume.

Quatre Ans de Captivité à Cochons-sur-Marne (Four Years of Captivity in Pigstye-on-the-Marne), 1900–1904. 3rd Diary.

L'Invendable (The Unsaleable), 1905–1907. 4th Diary.

Celle Qui Pleure (She Who Weeps), 1908.

Le Sang du Pauvre (The Poor Man's Blood), 1909.

Le Vieux de la Montagne (The Old Man of the Mountain), 1911. 5th Diary.

L'Ame de Napoléon (The Soul of Napoleon), 1912.

La Vie de Mélanie (The Life of Melanie), 1912.

Exegèse des Lieux Communs (Analysis of Stock-phrases), 1913. Volume 2.

Le Pélerin de l'Absolu (The Pilgrim of the Absolute), 1914. 6th Diary.

Jeanne d'Arc et l'Allemagne (Joan of Arc and Germany), 1915.

Au Seuil de l'Apocalypse (On the Threshold of the Apocalypse), 1916. 7th Diary.

Méditations d'un Solitaire (Meditations of a Solitary), 1916. 8th Diary.

Dans les Ténèbres (In the Shadows). Posthumous, 1918.

La Porte des Humbles (The Gateway of the Humble). Post. 1920.

Lettres à sa Fiancée (Letters to his Fiancée). Post. 1922.

Le Symbolisme de l'Apparition (The Symbolism of the Apparition), 1925.

Various Letters, 1920, 1927, 1935, 1937, 1945.

Principal Works of Léon Bloy